{ SHARING SECRETS }

A Conversation about the
Counterintuitive Nature of
Executive Leadership

ERIN SOTO

What people are saying about

{ SHARING SECRETS }

"For the first time, this book synthesizes three critical areas successful leaders must master: knowledge of proven leadership strategies, the good judgment that comes from years in the business, and acute self-awareness. Erin Soto gets you up to speed in all three areas in this highly accessible, simple-yet-brilliant book! I recommend Sharing Secrets to any new leader, or any leader want to make a new start!"

—MARSHALL GOLDSMITH
a Thinkers 50 Top Ten Global Business Thinker and top ranked executive coach.

"Erin is a natural leader who understands the guiding principle of transparency. Sharing Secrets is a great resource for aspiring leaders who endeavor to succeed."

—HENRIETTA FORE
former Administrator of the United States Agency for International Development and Director of U.S. Foreign Assistance and Chairman of the Board and Chief Executive Officer of Holsman International

"Sharing Secrets is a readable, practical roadmap for executive leaders in the public and private sectors. If I had Soto's wise advice, my adventure in executive leadership would have been more effective, productive and enjoyable. Sharing Secrets is a must read for all who aspire to successful careers in executive leadership positions."

—AMBASSADOR WILLIAM GARVELINK
Senior adviser for global strategy at the International Medical Corps and to the Center for Strategic and International Studies

"We all recognize a leader when we see one. But it is much less conspicuous to describe what it takes to lead. No single course, no particular book, no specific mentor can turn the aspiration to lead into an accomplished leader. But in her Sharing Secrets, author Erin Soto, take us up close and personal to some of leadership's required characteristics. Experienced leaders will be intrigued with Soto's insights while aspiring leaders will be both nourished and challenged. She liberally provides her readers access to the accumulation of observations (secrets) that her years of experience have afforded her. Read it; you will like it."

—DAN PELLEGROM
retired President of Pathfinder International and former Board Chair of InterAction

"A MUST READ for existing and aspiring senior executives -- one of the top five books on leadership, period. Erin Soto is a thinker, practitioner and real leader and now coach and advisor. She creates an easy-to-read, holistic and honest work in Sharing Secrets. Her book is a profound guide to thinking and cognitive exploration of self, others and organizations. Through personal anecdotes, colorful analogies and broad experiences, Erin talks about the demand by people and organizations for compassion, sincerity and truth. She upends common conventions as she discusses "counterintuitive" yet universal approaches to executive leadership, proven to work. Sharing Secrets should be on every leader's desk and in global boardrooms; if read widely it could change stoic, greedy and callous workplaces into more productive contributors to society. For those already pursuing a happier-productive workforce there are areas Erin Soto can help hone through exercises and checklists. Already looking forward to her next book!"

—GUS OTTO
former Professor of Practice of Strategic Leadership, National Defense University, Washington D.C.

"Sharing Secrets stands to impact the success rate of first-time executives. Erin details the job of the executive – what it is and what it isn't – and provides tools that will prepare the leader to succeed regardless of the sector or industry. This user-friendly book will help the executive optimize her time, lead with confidence and achieve balance."

—AMBASSADOR LEWIS LUCKE

"We need this book. Sharing Secrets is jam-packed with profound insights. Although geared toward aspiring and first-time executives, all leaders will benefit tremendously from Erin's Secret's. She shares with such humility and sincerity, one can't help but profit from her book."

—JENNIFER B. KAHNWEILER, PH.D.
Author of Quiet Influence and The Introverted Leader

"The key to success in leading at the executive level is in your hands. Erin Soto ably offers the experienced-based secrets and the harder to learn counterintuitive aspects so that you will be prepared to lead and set to succeed. Sharing Secrets is sure to inspire reflection in leaders and those aspiring to be leaders. It is useful for the personal and professional development of all who lead and serve."

—GERARD W. HALL, PH.D.
National Defense College, U.A.E

What people are saying about

{ SHARING SECRETS }

"More than ever before, organizational leaders must effectively manage for change and strategically communicate more than just good ideas and intent. Erin Soto's Sharing Secrets provides a practical and concise change management roadmap for senior managers across the business spectrum. As new leaders are being thrust into progressively more responsible positions and daily decision making challenges, this guidebook provides both necessary seasoning and sound advice. The author has the skill, wisdom and first hand experience to authoritatively state her case for Sharing Secrets' indispensable value to every leadership library."

—ALONZO FULGHAM
Senior Vice President International Development CH2M Hill and former Acting Administrator USAID

"Full of practical advice for immediate use! Written with wisdom and complete vulnerability, Sharing Secrets provides a roadmap for implementing the critical aspects of great leadership. Anchoring each focus area with real life experiences and proven research, Erin highlights dozens of steps to guide the new leader and aid the veteran senior leader. Few government or business executives have the courage to share their insights the way she has in Sharing Secrets."

—KATHY KNAPP
President of K2 Leadership Group, LLC, and Former Chair of the Strategic Leadership Department, National Defense University

"In *Sharing Secrets* leadership expert Erin Soto shares with us a beautifully written integration of practical executive leadership lessons that are underpinned by academic research. An immensely valuable volume for new and experienced leaders alike."

—JEFFREY E. AUERBACH, PhD, MCC,
President, College of Executive Coaching, A Post-Graduate Insitute, Past Vice-President, International Coach Federation Global Board of Directors

"Secrets come in many forms. The reader will find some that are crystal clear and others that are more nuanced, but I found each and every one that is shared in this book to be true and useful. Many insights that I learned slowly over years appeared familiarly on the page in front of me, alongside others that sparked many "aha moments." Sharing Secrets is an "executive accelerator" and I would bet that nearly every executive who reads this book will find ways to quickly improve approaches, techniques and results; moreover, those improvements will have lasting effects that will benefit those executives and their colleagues and their organizations for years to come."

—LAURENCE M. DAY, PhD, MPH
President and CEO, CAMRIS International

Printed in the United States of America.
For information, address TLC Solutions, LLC
3008 North Rochester Street, Arlington, VA 22213

Front cover design and interior layout by Nick Isabella.

ISBN-13: 978-0692291245

TLC Solutions, LLC
Leader Development Services

This book is dedicated to my mother, Maryalyce Truman McDavid who always said, "Speak from your heart and you cannot go wrong." To my father, Dr. Robert F. McDavid, who said, "Progress is not always in a straight line." And, most especially to Ben Soto, my partner for dancing through life.

"Every day we slaughter our finest impulses. That is
why we get a heart-ache when we read those lines
written by the hand of a master and recognize them as
our own, as the tender shoots which we stifled because
we lacked the faith to believe in our own powers,
our own criterion of truth and beauty. Every man,
when he gets quiet, when he becomes desperately
honest with himself, is capable of uttering profound
truths. We all derive from the same source. There is
no mystery about the origin or things. We are all part
of creation, all kings, all poets, all musicians; we have
only to open up, to discover what is already there."

—HENRY MILLER
Sexus

{ TABLE OF CONTENTS }

Foreword i

Acknowledgements v

Introduction vii

Part I

Chapter One: *It Doesn't Look Like Work!* 1

Chapter Two: *Invest in Your People* 15

Chapter Three: *Keeping Up with the Joneses* 29

Chapter Four: *All Systems Go!* 41

Chapter Five: *Draw the Map* 55

Chapter Six: *Bridge the Gap* 71

Chapter Seven: *The Mother of All Systems* 91

Chapter Eight: *Talk to Me!* 105

Chapter Nine: *Only the Wicked Problems Please* 123

Chapter Ten: *Yes, You Can Have Work-Life Balance!* 141

Chapter Eleven: *Reflect, Learn, Grow!* 157

Part II

Chapter Twelve: *Are You Ready to Lead?* 171

Chapter Thirteen: *The Floor of Executive Performance* 181

Chapter Fourteen: *Go Team Go!* 201

Chapter Fifteen: *Ready to Lead and Set to Succeed!* 215

Conclusion: *The Path Traveled* 231

About the Author I

Bibliography III

Footnotes IX

{ FOREWORD }

by Jennifer L. Windsor

Sharing Secrets is a refreshingly honest and imminently practical guide for those who want to succeed in executive leadership positions. The book covers the gamut of issues that an executive leader must grapple with—strategy setting, organizational culture, staff development and motivation, communication, time allocation—while avoiding the jargon and repetitiveness that so often plague other books on leadership and management. Each chapter discusses key facets of leadership, drawing on concrete examples based on Erin Soto's extensive experiences as a manager and leader, and her astute observations about the various executives she has worked for and with over the years. Throughout the book, readers will find opportunities to reflect upon and evaluate their own experiences, traits, and challenges.

Reading through it, I found myself nodding in agreement, underlining points and insights that resonated with my own experience as an executive in the government, non-profit, and university sectors over the past 20 years. When I finished it, I thought about how useful it would have been to read this book before my first experience leading the Democracy Center in the 1990s, during the decade I spent as Executive Director of Freedom House, or when I was an Associate Dean at the

School of Foreign Service at Georgetown. Perhaps I might have made fewer mistakes. But as Erin reiterates throughout the book, part of being a great executive leader is admitting and then learning from the mistakes that we all inevitably make.

Indeed, what is most powerful about this book, and what makes it stand out among others, is Erin's willingness to share "secrets" that go beyond traditional management topics. She writes eloquently and persuasively about the need for leaders to embrace their vulnerability, acknowledge their fallibility, and reveal their essential humanness. Leaders who are authentic, who leads with their hearts as well as lead their minds, are leaders who can inspire trust and loyalty in those who work for them. Staff development, as Erin notes, is not simply about training and promotions; staff learn from how executives lead, how they spend their time, and how they conduct themselves every day. Great leaders spend more time listening than speaking. They engage broadly by seeking input, not imposing top-down changes while guiding the organization towards greater effectiveness. Great leaders make only those decisions that others cannot make and base decisions on relevant information and rigorous and systematic reviews of assumptions, data, and implications. They genuinely care about those who work for them. For Erin, the decision to work reasonable hours, to spend time with friends and family, and to care for oneself is not a luxury, it is a necessity for great leadership. It helps both the leader and the organization to succeed. These are revolutionary ideas—ideas, which if followed, could help transform the nature of the workplace in the United States, a transformation that many believe is long overdue.

I had the great privilege to work with Erin when we both were founding members of the then newly formed Democracy Center at USAID. She impressed me with her professionalism, her willingness to work hard, and her obvious intelligence. I have watched with respect and admiration as she moved up in the leadership ranks, including serving as a mission director in two complex countries, Cambodia and India. But nothing has impressed me more than Erin's writing of this book. It is brimming full of practical tips and nuggets of wisdom for aspiring leaders. The way Erin writes is the clearest demonstration of the kind of courageous and compassionate leader and executive coach that Erin Soto has become.

—JENNIFER L. WINDSOR
Washington, DC
August 19, 2014

{ ACKNOWLEDGEMENTS }

Thank you to women and men of the US Agency for International Development and Department of State—the peacemakers—those who are making this world a better, safer place to live. They rarely get recognized for the heroic work they do day in and day out. Many examples used in the book were drawn from my USAID career and include people who have had a tremendous impact on my career and leadership. Thank you to them all for being good examples of positive leadership. They include: Jim Kunder, Lew Lucke, Patrick Robinson, Padu Padmanaban, Hillary Clinton, Steve Gaffney, Bob McDavid, Dave Eckerson, Chuck Costello, Olivier Carduner, Jenny Vernooy, Bill Gelman, Leslie Reed, Uzra Zeya, George Deikun, Alex Newton, Jeff Harris, Helene Gayle, Jennifer Windsor, Debra McFarland, Gary Hansen, and Jerry Hyman, Ann Van Dusen, Sally Shelton Colby, Mary Tarnowka, Jennifer Adams, Lisa Franchette, Henrietta Fore, Kate Crawford, Bernadette Bundy Mitchell, Josie Fritsch, Liz Warfield, Don Lu, Tim Roemer, Alonzo Fulgrum, Pat Ramsey, Mosina Jordan, Bill Garvelink, Richard Roth, Rob Jackson, Alejandro Vassilaqui, Pape Sow, Anna Diallo, Tom Delaney, Julie Klement, and Neil Levine.

Something as daunting of an undertaking as writing a book is never achieved without a whole host of friends and family cheering you on along the way. Thank you to my entire family, Kathryn Viguerie, Rob and Kerstin Mockrish, Arielle Jean-Baptist, Bridget Collins, Neil Levine, Sharon Bean, and Tami Halmrast-Sanchez as well as Ben, Maggie and Pedro, of course.

Although my name goes on the cover, writing a book is the work of many, many people who often contribute behind the scenes. Thank you to Kathy Knapp for opening the first door to writing the book. Marshall Goldsmith who generously offered guiding words and helpful resources as I began the process of writing the book. Kelly Bennett, my coach who provided the cornerstone to the entire book writing experience. Sarah McArthur, my editor extraordinaire without her there would be no book to share. Maggie Soto who patiently and accurately transcribed hours of voice recordings and keyed in dozens of edits. Pedro Soto who assisted with layout design. Ed McDavid, my New York copy editor with a keen eye for detail. Nick Isabella who so creatively designed the book graphics. Kathlyn Hyatt Stewart who carefully combed the manuscript to enhance the credibility and value of the book. Becky Robinson and her team for providing expert promotion services and guidance. I thank them all for their work in making *Sharing Secrets*.

{ INTRODUCTION }

"**D**o you want to dance?"

It was a Friday night. The lights were low and the place was buzzing with college students and young adults meeting after a week of work and study. Drinks were flowing. The music was pulsing and the urge to dance was omnipresent. A young man—tall, dark, and handsome— approached me and asked in a barely audible, accented voice, "Do you want to dance?" This simple question, asked millions of times around the world every day, has a straightforward, inconsequential answer. Or does it? In my case, a "yes" response to this question resulted in a lifelong secret that significantly handicapped my leadership abilities until it was finally revealed. Holding some secrets can damage your ability to lead. A few years later, a "yes" response to this question resulted in life-altering positive consequences that proved invaluable to me as a leader. Same question, same answer, and both revealed to me surprising secrets of success for executive leaders as well as lessons for life.

Executive leadership is not rocket science. It is a savvy combination of art and science. Even with training, though, it can feel like driving without a dashboard, at best, or piloting an airplane for the first time through a thunderstorm without flight instruments, at worst. Methods, approaches, and tools that worked well at lower levels don't work as well, if at all, at the executive level. If you are a successful executive leader now, you know, and if you are on track to become an executive leader you will soon find out, that the tools and techniques for success at the executive leadership level are not the same as those at other leadership levels.

Sharing Secrets is about leading at the executive level. In this book, I talk about three kinds of secrets. The first secrets are approaches and procedures that have stood the test of time. These are experience-based secrets. Academics and seasoned professionals have written books and published articles about certain aspects of executive leadership. This book spans the full complement of these aspects and demonstrates how these secrets can augment your conceptual framework for leading at the executive level. The job of an executive leader is fundamentally different from that of leaders at other levels; as such, the requirements of the job are different. It is important to understand what your job is, what it is not, and the boundaries of your position.

The second type of secrets are a subset of experienced-based secrets, which emerge only after leading at the executive level and often after making mistakes. These are secrets that are counterintuitive in nature. Because these secrets are not intuitive, they are less obvious, harder to learn, and more difficult to adopt. They are also more difficult to teach or convey. Some leaders never fully understand these secrets. I believe that this lack of understanding accounts for the high failure rate among new executives.

Last and perhaps most importantly, the third type of secrets are those past events or traits that fear keeps tucked away and hidden from view, but that profoundly impact your leadership ability. Let's call these personal secrets. Sharing these secrets goes beyond divulging your mistakes as a leader. It means knowing yourself, dealing with your fears, and sharing those personal secrets that are holding you back from being your authentic self and achieving your potential.

In order to share such information, you must be vulnerable, and being so contributes to developing a humility that naturally attracts others. Vulnerability is equally, if not more, important than other characteristics of great leaders. Thus, you become a leader who people choose to follow. This likely sounds counterintuitive to you as you walk the road of being a "successful leader," and it is. But like much of what you are going to learn in these pages, it is critical, because being a great leader isn't as straightforward as it seems; neither are the component parts of leadership. Without sharing these secrets, you can't make yourself vulnerable, and vulnerability is key to building trust. Without trust, you won't build the following that you need to achieve the vision and goals you are charged with executing as an executive leader. Sharing secrets—experience-based, counterintuitive, and personal—is absolutely essential for your success.

Such sharing is not viewed as a positive trait, and it is certainly not at the top of most lists of "mandatory" or "essential" executive traits. Instead, vulnerability is seen as a weakness. Because of this view, most of us attempt to hide our flaws and don't discuss our mistakes. We prefer to forget and certainly don't reveal our embarrassing moments, we don't talk about our weaknesses or embrace our imperfections, and we don't reach out for help. As a result, these all become pushed underground, hidden.

It takes tremendous effort to hold these kinds of secrets. If held over many years, these secrets change the way we interact with others. We worry about what others might think of us if they knew our secrets. Fear of disclosure grips us and we avoid even the hint of possibility of exposure—whether that means not taking a leadership position, limiting our social circles, hedging certain tasks, or avoiding certain friends and family.

Yet, until we share our secrets, until we know and disclose our true selves, face our fears, and become vulnerable by revealing ourselves, flaws and all, we will never be the great leaders we are capable of becoming. Though this seems counterintuitive, it works like this:

when we are vulnerable, we become more genuine, and empathetic to others—more appealing, more relatable. We become approachable and people want to develop relationships with us. They want to follow us.

The Secrets of Becoming a Great Leader

Why isn't being a great leader straightforward? First, leaders are not adequately trained to be successful executives. They generally have to "learn on the job." Adults typically learn by making mistakes, by reflecting, asking for feedback, and then adjusting appropriately. The catch is that at the most senior ranks, no one wants to acknowledge mistakes or that they need help for fear of being viewed as incompetent or "in over their heads." Surfacing these mistakes feels tantamount to career suicide. With heightened competition for executive talent and internal promotions, letting on that you have made a mistake or need help feels risky.

Further, while executive leadership is learned largely by experience and by making mistakes, most executives aren't comfortable discussing their errors. So, ironically, it is difficult for them to pass on their learnings to the next generation. These "best practices" are filed away in their memories and become secrets. Secrets, that if you knew them, could significantly raise your awareness and enhance your chances of success as an executive leader.

This book endeavors to share those secrets. Some of the nearly three dozen experienced-based secrets you will learn are:

- Executives know that thinking is a critical part of their job and reserve time every day for reflecting, alone, without exception.

- Executives allow for failure as an explicit tactic of growing talent.

- Executives make only the decisions that others cannot make. They focus their decisions at the strategic and systemic levels.

- Executives' leadership styles are one of the biggest recruiting tactics for any company or organization.

In addition to the many experienced-based secrets of successful executive leadership, this book will examine the many ways that successful executive leaders act counterintuitively. The counterintuitive secrets are not straightforward. This is, in part, what makes leading at the executive level so difficult to master. What does counterintuitive look like? My first experience with it was as a 14-year-old athlete. I ran the mile—not very fast but I ran it. It was the first year my school allowed girls to run the mile. My father was an exercise physiologist and he encouraged me to run negative splits: you run the first half of your race slower than the last half, capitalizing on the physiology of the human body. When the gun goes off at the start of the race, you hang back. You are possibly at the end of the pack for the first half of the race. When you want to win, that is a hard place to be. But you do it because you understand how your body operates optimally for longer distances. When you sprint, your body enters oxygen debt after about 40 seconds. When this process begins, your body operates suboptimally and fatigue sets in quickly. When using negative splits, you have the reserves necessary to pick up your pace and end the race with a winning sprint. Running negative splits is counterintuitive and hard to do, because it takes practice to hold back and trust that by doing so you will have the reserves to kick past the others to victory in the second half of the race.

Executive leadership is similar in that sometimes you hold back from jumping in, giving direction, or solving the problem. You trust that a method other than your own might work better in the long run. It is difficult to hold back and it takes practice to master the method of thinking and acting counterintuitively. However, understanding the counterintuitive nature of these new tools and techniques and the rationale behind them is a good first step toward adopting them. These tools and techniques are also secrets, the counterintuitive secrets, of success at the executive level. Here are a few examples of over a dozen counterintuitive secrets that will be discussed in the book:

- When they are pressed for time and need or want rapid change, executives move slowly.

- Executives gain control by loosening the reins and empowering staff.

- Executives promote collaboration, understanding that it is a more effective strategy than competition for achieving and sustaining long-term results.

- Executives know that ownership is infinite and share credit with everyone, even those who may not deserve it.

Why I Wrote This Book

We aren't getting it right yet! A study from the Center for Creative Leadership in Greensboro, North Carolina, found that 40% of executives who had changed jobs or gotten promoted failed in the first 18 months. Likewise, Kevin Kelly, CEO of Heidrick & Struggles, a leading executive search firm, pointed to Heidrick's internal study which found that 40% of executives hired at the senior level were pushed out, failed, or quit within 18 months. Batting .400 in baseball is good, but it is horrible in leadership, particularly when assuming stewardship of millions and billions of dollars and the lives of hundreds of thousands and millions of employees. Couple that with the fact that the average age of executive leaders has dropped. Well-known leadership development experts, Michael Watkins and Peter Daly claim that 250,000 public-sector management positions turn over every year. Tenures for executive leaders—especially in the private sector—are shorter now than before. There is increased pressure to move quickly, yet a lower tolerance for errors. Crushing pressure from the media weighs on top executive leaders. Employees cite a lack of leadership near the top of their concerns and few executive leaders believe that they were adequately trained for their positions. As executive leaders, we haven't fully understood these trends and are not yet equipped to counter them. In writing *Sharing Secrets*, I hope to contribute to understanding these trends as a first step toward impacting them.

Sharing Secrets endeavors to offer explanations and help to leaders in countering these trends. By the time you reach the last pages of this book, you will have a comprehensive conceptual framework for leading at the executive level in any public- or private-sector position. You will know the secrets to becoming a distinguished leader. You will have expanded your repertoire of tips, tools, and strategies for success. Put succinctly, you will be ready to lead and set to succeed.

Many academics write books on leadership from a social scientific perspective. They make important contributions to help fuel practitioners with scientific knowledge. Many practitioners write books describing their personal stories and special recipes for success. Sharing Secrets is different in that it combines my nearly 30 years of practical leadership experience in the public and international arenas, including a decade in the executive ranks, with the academic underpinnings found in universities. This book uniquely synthesizes these two distinct perspectives to create new ways of understanding executive leadership and preparing rising or new executives.

As an experienced executive, I taught executive leadership at the National Defense University to master's students from government, private, and international arenas who were on the brink of executive leadership positions. As a development expert for nearly 30 years, I worked the majority of my career for the United States Agency for International Development, (USAID), the part of the federal government that provides support to developing nations in a way that promotes democracy, good governance, and economic prosperity. I served in senior and executive positions for more than a decade. I retired as a career member of the Senior Foreign Service, the executive corps of the Foreign Service. Over the course of my career, I have lived and worked in seven developing countries (Guatemala, Mali, Senegal, Haiti, Peru, Cambodia, and India) and traveled to dozens of others. I draw on all of these experiences in writing this book.

In addition, I model the vulnerability I promote as so crucial to executive success by sharing my mistakes, as well as my triumphs. And, I divulge some of my own hidden secrets that were impeding my leadership in hopes that you will find the courage to do the same.

I've written *Sharing Secrets* because I want to help prepare the next generation of leaders to be better at leading than I was. The issues and problems they face will most certainly be more complex. Increasing global elements in the workplace will, by definition, enhance the complexity of leading people and tackling problems. Even if you aren't an executive leader, by understanding aspects of the executive's job relative to your own, you can learn to better support and have a more positive relationship with your leader, as well as prepare yourself for executive leadership positions in the future.

The Structure of the Book

This book is written in two parts: In Part I, Chapter One, I outline the job of an executive leader and surface the counterintuitive aspects. In Chapters Two through Eleven, I explore the key aspects of an executive leader's job, including external and internal assessments, vision and strategy, culture, change agenda, communication, making executive decisions, taking care of oneself, reflecting, synthesizing, and allowing for contingencies. Each chapter covers what the responsibilities of the executive are and are not, and provides examples, charts, tools, and tips to understand the job and do it well. Believe it or not, many people in executive positions spend a lot of time doing things that simply aren't their responsibility. By the end of Part I, you will be clear about the parameters of your job and be able to approximate about how much time you should spend on each component. You will be armed with secrets and tips to carry out your job well. You'll have insights into the counterintuitive nature of these components of your job. In short, you will be equipped with the knowledge you need to succeed at the executive level.

Part II is designed to ensure that you are fully prepared to lead. Information about leader readiness in Chapter Twelve, leadership styles in Chapter Thirteen, and high-performing teams in Chapter Fourteen will amply prepare you for an executive leadership position. Chapter Fifteen details the first crucial steps in the career of an executive leader, especially a first-time executive leader. It will set you on the path to great leadership.

Sharing Secrets is full of stories and cases of both good and poor leadership. The depiction of poor leaders is not meant to incriminate or blame, but rather designed for all of us to learn from and grow. The contrast between good and poor leadership is a way for you, as a leader, to assess yourself and to see where you fall on the continuum of executive leadership.

Ultimately, an executive leader's job is to develop people. The best executives understand this and practice it day in and day out. They know that amazing results will follow if they invest in their people, that all of their expectations will be exceeded if they simply take care of their people and help them grow and learn.

My hope in writing this book is that it will help executives, aspiring executives, and high potentials become great leaders and show the necessity for all of us to help each other become successful if we are to be truly successful ourselves. I also hope this book strengthens your conceptual framework about leadership and, indeed, about people and life. Read on and discover the secrets that no one has shared with you before about what it takes to succeed at the highest levels of your company, your organization, or your government!

—ERIN SOTO
Washington D.C.

{ PART I }

Chapter One

{ IT DOESN'T LOOK LIKE WORK! }

You've made it to the senior ranks. You are a well-respected, driven, intelligent achiever. You've worked hard to get to this level. Long days and weekends are finally going to pay off. Your paycheck is bigger. You'll have command over your schedule and can keep normal hours. The support for your position is greater. You may even have a driver. You probably have an executive assistant who runs your errands, keeps your schedule, and helps you to avoid missing birthdays. You probably don't know everyone in your company or organization. You will spend more time in the public eye speaking to larger groups. You will likely travel a lot more. You'll have access to senior peers and captains of industry with whom you'll wine and dine. It sounds wonderful, doesn't it? Easy even: it sounds like a dream job.

The reality is that executive leadership is anything but easy. It is hard, really hard. It doesn't always look like work, but it is. All of a sudden you have to be all things to all people. The demands on your time are enormous. Expectations are impossible to meet. Mistakes are visible to your peers, your superiors, and the public. They cost the organization money and they have the potential to damage your reputation and even end your career. Your decisions are consequential and impact an order of magnitude greater than what you have dealt with before. The stakes are high and the pressure is immense. You bear full responsibility for your organization, company, or institution.

What Is Your Job as an Executive?

If you don't thoroughly understand what your job is and what it isn't, you will likely be derailed, pushed aside, or replaced. Successful executive leadership starts and ends with understanding your scope. There is a reason to have a clear demarcation, a threshold to cross, between executive-level leaders and other leaders. The reason is that, unlike lower-level leaders, you are responsible for bringing value to improve the competitiveness of your company or the effectiveness of your organization: Full stop. It sounds simple. It is, of course, not. Repeat this out loud:

"My goal is to improve the competitiveness of _____*."*
(if you are in the private sector)

"My goal is to improve the effectiveness of _____*."*
(if you are in the public sector)

One of the statements above is your bull's eye (depending upon whether the organization you are leading is part of the private or public sector). It is what all your actions and decisions should be focused on achieving.

When you take an executive leadership position, you will likely receive direction from the board, CEO, secretary, or president. If you are lucky, that direction is explicit, e.g., increase market share by 4%, take three new products through the proof-of-concept phase, or reduce costs in shipping by 7%. More than likely, however, the direction will be more general and full of ambiguity. You will get orders like, "fix the mess," "turn the ship around," and "beef up research and development." Don't be confused. Your job is either to increase the competitiveness of your company or the effectiveness of your organization by bringing your value to bear. Your value is your intelligence, training, experience, interpersonal skills, time, and networks. Your value should increase the competitiveness of the company or the effectiveness of the organization. How you apply your value is as important as your value itself. You have to bring clarity and certainty to the ambiguity you have been handed.

Your job is not to have all the answers, to make all the decisions, or to control all the aspects of the enterprise. This is, perhaps, where the counterintuitive nature of executive leadership begins. Making decisions and getting results is probably what you've done to get to the top, but this approach won't work now because your job is fundamentally different. Your number one priority now is to develop your people. You apply your value through your people. Again, though it sounds simple, it is anything but.

Your time is a key asset of the company or institution you are leading. Think of it as an investment that should have big payoffs. It is a significant part of your value to the organization, and how you spend your time indicates to subordinates what you and the organization value. It's also an indicator of how well you know your job and a consequence of this knowledge, i.e., how well you can lead. Let's review in more detail how you should spend your time.

Executive Time Distribution

Let's first take a look at how executives should spend their time
(see Table 1.1):

Table 1.1: Executive Time Distribution			
	Executive Role	**Time Spent**	**Sharing Secrets Chapter(s)**
1	Investing in staff growth and development	10%	Chapter 2
2	Assessing the external and internal environments to shape the vision and strategy	60%	Chapters 3, 4, 5
3	Communicating to stakeholders to guide the change agenda	10%	Chapters 6, 7, 8
4	Making decisions of consequence	5%	Chapter 9
5	Taking care of yourself	5%	Chapter 10
6	Reflecting, analyzing, and synthesizing information	5%	Chapter 11
7	Allowing time for contingencies and unexpected events	5%	Chapter 11

1. Investing in Staff Growth and Development

In interviews with executives, from CEOs to ambassadors to directors of major programs, I've found that there is a general consensus that if you take care of your people, help them develop and grow, the results will come, expectations will be exceeded, your company will be more competitive, and your organization will be more effective. These day-to-day investments in your people may not yield growth immediately. A delayed return on investment, coupled with the relatively short tenure of executives, make staff development counterintuitive perhaps, but without such investment, there will not be competitiveness and effectiveness.

"Develop your people? What do you mean? I send them to training, isn't that enough? What if they make mistakes? Should I just let them fail?" The answer to these questions varies, and this is the art of leadership. The best thing you can do is set a good example. Then empower your people to make decisions. Finally, allow space for mistakes; this is how people learn.

While investing in staff growth and development is job number one, it should occupy only about 10% of an executive's time. This "time spent" is a bit deceiving, because developing staff is indirectly reflected in how the executive conducts himself, in the way he makes decisions, and in the degree of transparency he exhibits in decision making, how communication flows, and so on. Among the very best executives, investing in staff growth and development holds the highest priority of all functions of the job, superseding all other elements. Investing in staff development includes mentoring through complex tasks, modeling positive skills and traits, coaching through stretch assignments and meeting regularly to discuss staff's growth and development.

Perhaps the biggest recruiting tactic is how you lead your company or organization. Word gets out. If you are known as an executive who develops and invests in staff, provides opportunities for growth, and allows people space to create, you will attract followers. If you consciously create a work environment that values both work-life balance and teamwork, these elements will be a powerful recruitment tool. People yearn to work for great leaders. Your actions and your leadership can be important factors in both recruiting and retaining talent.

2. Assessing the External and Internal Environments to Shape the Vision and Strategy

This may surprise you, but leaders at the top of an organization should spend a minimum of 60% of their time gathering information and engaging with people outside of the organization. While it may not look like work, the external networks executives build are critical to achieving their internal objectives.

In your executive leadership position, you will tap into your network of peers, captains of industry, and leaders of governments to obtain the best information possible to enable you to make the decisions that no one else can make. If you are to do this successfully, you must build trust between and among your networks.

You will spend a lot of time gathering information about trends or external forces that could impact your company or organization, as well as information about your competitors. You will analyze and synthesize this information with an aim toward predicting and shaping the future. Synthesizing this information is the basis for establishing a vision for the future and, equally important, a strategy for fulfilling that vision.

Similarly, executives need to have a finger on the pulse of their own company or organization. They must assess the internal environment and, in particular, the internal systems, focusing on determining the extent to which internal systems are aligned with each other and are consistent with the values of the company or organization. They must ensure that all internal systems support the overarching vision and strategy. They strive for systems that are lean and efficient. This kind of internal assessment takes a tremendous amount of time.

3. Communicating to Stakeholders to Guide the Change Agenda

As you draw conclusions from your assessment of both external forces and internal systems, you establish a vision and strategy. The gaps between where you are and where you want to be encompass the change agenda—the steps needed to bring internal systems into greater alignment with each other and with the overall vision and strategy. This change can be almost anything. For instance, you may see that the reward system is out of sync with the teamwork environment your company needs to achieve the kind of innovation that is required to remain competitive. In government, you may see new initiatives that are out of sync with budget systems or skill sets. The job of the executive, then, is to strive for greater alignment of the internal systems that support the larger vision and strategy.

In striving for such alignment, you'll find that the mother of all systems is the culture. Corporate culture is a strong and powerful internal force. Because it is invisible, it is sometimes difficult to assess; however, the executive who ignores culture won't achieve her objectives. Culture is that powerful. Questions arise initially, such as, should you assimilate to the culture or have the culture assimilate to your leadership style? That is jumping ahead! While shaping culture is an important element of your job and part of the larger change agenda, it takes a long time to change it. Additionally, before you can change a culture, you must understand it.

When communicating internally, you will want to tap into the existing, culturally appropriate means of communicating, at least initially. How you communicate is as important as what you communicate.

Essentially, your job as an executive is to communicate the vision and strategy of the organization and to relate successes to multiple audiences with varied frequency. You should spend about 10% of your time communicating. You will communicate with stakeholders both outside and inside the company or organization. External stakeholders include competitors, collaborators, and cooperators. Internal stakeholders can be the board of directors, peers, and staff at the edge of the enterprise. The communication can be one-on-one or to thousands. It can be face-to-face or through social media and the internet.

Most executives believe that they are communicating both more frequently and more effectively than they actually are. In reality, they may be speaking, but not communicating. As a result, subordinates often cite a lack of communication from their leaders as a chief complaint. Great leaders communicate with clarity and frequency. They have connected and earned the trust of those with whom they communicate. They listen closely and empathetically. They are able to tailor messages readily and effectively. They are patient as they communicate their message over and over until it is heard, understood, and acted upon; until the change is bought and owned. Communicating the change agenda, whether the change is an aspect of culture, developing a major new product line, or

:o collaborate rather than compete, is a fundamental element
:cutive's job.

Measures of great leadership are not always tangible and quan-
tifiable, but also include intangibles that are difficult to measure, such
as trust, team spirit, pride, and love. These are the factors that distinguish good from great leaders who lead by investing in their people and
who understand their most important job: develop their people. These
attributes play a catalytic role in innovation and solving the complex
problems that are so key to competitiveness and effectiveness. You can
judge a leader by the atmosphere she creates through communication.
Yet this atmosphere is hard to measure. Perhaps because it is hard
to measure, it doesn't get measured often. And because it doesn't get
measured, people afford it lower importance. It is counterintuitive in
that it doesn't seem important, but is of paramount importance.

4. Making Decisions of Consequence

Executives spend time about 5% of their time making decisions,
but not just any decisions. They focus on those decisions that subordinates cannot make. Typically, the more complex and consequential
decisions are reserved for the executive. Consequential means that a
decision impacts the strategy and/or large numbers of people. Executives must relinquish control of decisions of lesser consequence. This is
counterintuitive. At the executive level, loose is tight. What do I mean
by that? I mean, you must give up control. You cannot possibly make all
the decisions that you made previously plus the ones required of you at
the executive level. You may be great at making decisions at the lower
level, but many roads lead to the same results, and your decision, your
road, is but one way to get there. Other people will take other roads. It
is important to allow subordinates to travel the roads they choose and
assess whether there is a shortcut, a better way, a faster route, a better
decision. This is how they learn and develop. This is one very important
way that you fulfill your most important role, developing your people.
And, more importantly, relinquishing control gives you more power,
because it builds trust. If you trust your subordinates, they will trust

you. They will follow you. So decision making is part of the executive's job, but only a select set of decisions should be yours to make.

Again, it is counterintuitive, but executives are not supposed to have all the answers. In fact, it turns out that it isn't advisable for them to have all the answers. If you have all the answers, you leave no space for the engagement of others in making a decision and you increase your liability. You run the risk of being wrong because you didn't understand a nuance or a detail. One of the first things executives have to understand is that not only are they not expected to have all the answers, it is disastrous for them to pretend to have all the answers. As soon as you realize this, your life will become much simpler. You may even feel as if a weight has been lifted off your shoulders.

Know Your Job!

An executive's time is a key investment for a company or organization. Every executive should ensure that he knows his job and uses his time wisely. If you find yourself doing any of the following, unless you are an extremely small business or organization, you are probably not investing your time as wisely as you could. An executive leader must avoid these kinds of tasks: editing documents or communications products; making decisions below the vision and strategy level (technical or tactical level); reviewing data below the system level (subsystem level) unless there is an issue. To the extent that you are spending time on these things, you are either not carrying out the responsibilities of your executive position or you are trying to do too many tasks at once. If you are trying to do both tactical or subsystem level tasks as well as strategic and system level tasks, I guarantee something will give. Either you will fail as a leader in the form of a serious professional crisis, or your health, family, or marriage will suffer. The solution to this problem is as simple as knowing what your job is and isn't.

5. *Taking Care of Yourself*

It is important to spend time every day taking care of yourself. To ensure your highest productivity, spend some time daily doing something that relaxes you like cooking, playing bridge, singing, acting, reading, or exercising. Research indicates that even with mild and acute stress the there is a dramatic loss of cognitive abilities.[1] Outside hobbies and regular physical activity aids in stress management. As you are called on to make decisions that have serious consequences for your company or organization, stress management for an executive is exponentially important. Five percent of your time during the workday should be spent on activities to reduce stress and while you're not likely to spend work time on your hobbies, you can have a relaxing lunch, go for a walk, read, and schedule five minutes between meetings to gather your thoughts, for example, during the workday. Also, in developing staff, modeling stress management is especially valuable. If you take the time to take care of yourself, those whom you lead may feel justified in doing the same and this will positively impact the productivity and quality of work across the board.

Part of taking care of yourself is establishing behaviors and boundaries that ensure work-life balance. Reject the "do whatever it takes" attitude. Pay attention to the warning signs of working excessively. Know yourself and your values and align them with your career goals to heighten the possibility of success. Ensure that you are fully prepared to lead at the executive level and you can have work-life balance and so can those who work with you.

6. *Reflecting, Analyzing, and Synthesizing Information*

Executives should spend some time every day reflecting. Again, this may not look like work, but good executives spend about 30 minutes every day thinking—not multitasking—just thinking…about their decisions, their people and teams, and their communications.

Too many conversations in the workplace are ad hoc and hinge on moods, energy levels, relationships, and personalities.[2] You see it every day. In an hour-long meeting, even if there is an agenda, a facilitator, and an objective, the conversation is often unstructured and characterized by long arguments and personality clashes. Participants don't reveal their true feelings. Ideas are presented in a haphazard manner and lack clarity or detail. Assumptions are silently made without discussion. As an executive leader, you can manage this with prior reflection.

Reflect on the conversations you plan to have. Be deliberate in what you want to convey and the purpose for it. When you engage, demand that other people express themselves in a coherent and clear fashion. Sometimes that, in and of itself, is a mountain to climb. People haven't been taught how to express themselves or to put together an argument. It takes work, but over time, conversations will become more meaningful, relationships will become more solid, and trust will be built.

During your daily reflection period, you'll want to spend time thinking about trends and strategy. You should be thinking about today, tomorrow, and 20 to 30 years from now. Reflecting is when learning happens, insights occur, and growth flourishes.

7. Allowing Time for Contingencies and Unexpected Events

This is straightforward, although few executives actually carve out time every day for the unforeseen issues that inevitably arise. If you've accurately assessed and synthesized information from stakeholders and assessed internal systems; if you've got a vision, realistic strategy, and a change agenda that your team owns; and if you trust and empower your staff, then there should be few unexpected events. However, they do happen, and happen fairly regularly. Then there are major events that are unforeseen. It is difficult to plan for a natural disaster that disrupts your entire business model, ideological political fights that shut down government, or a large-scale security event or accident.

Most large companies and certainly the government have plans in place should these types of major events occur. However, when your day is consistently thrown off schedule because of unforeseen events or you are spending large percentages of your time dealing with the fallout of such events, this may be an indicator of a larger problem. Perhaps you didn't accurately assess the external environment to detect trends and patterns and account for them in your vision or strategy. Perhaps your assessment of internal systems indicated a greater degree of alignment than actually exists. The ideal is to spend less than 5% of your time on these kinds of issues, which means that you can spend more time on your number one priority, investing in staff development and growth; spending more than 5% calls for a reassessment.

Summary

Executive leadership isn't easy. One way to make it more manageable is to understand precisely what your job is and what it is not. This chapter has detailed the responsibilities of the executive, the time that should be spent on these responsibilities, and offered examples to help you gain a fuller understanding of the executive leader's job. In the following chapters, I will discuss each of these items in greater detail and depth.

Chapter One Secrets

1. Know your top goal: You are responsible for bringing value to improve the competitiveness of your company or the effectiveness of your organization.

2. Your job is not to have all the answers, to make all the decisions, or to control all the aspects of the enterprise.

3. The best leaders view their time as an asset and invest their time to yield the greatest value to the institution. They are disciplined in daily reflection.

4. Staff growth and development is job number one of an executive.

5. Great leaders relinquish control of decisions of lesser consequence.

6. Putting yourself above other priorities is key to ensuring your highest productivity.

Chapter One Exercise

Write down the precise parameters of your job. Review the components of time distribution in this chapter. Then, track your own time allocation to determine how close you are to the ideal distribution.

Chapter Two

$\left\{\begin{array}{c}\end{array}\right.$ # INVEST IN YOUR PEOPLE $\left.\begin{array}{c}\end{array}\right\}$

A dmiral Mike Mullen, a retired Navy admiral and Chairman of the Joint Chiefs of Staff from 2007 to 2011, was the highest ranking military officer in the United States and is an extremely well-respected leader. He was appointed to four different four-star assignments in service to our country, something only two other leaders in history have achieved. In a television interview on his leadership style, Admiral Mullen indicated that he leads by listening, learning, and seeing problems through other people's eyes. His advice to aspiring leaders: know your people and take care of them.[3]

In 2007, I went to Cambodia to head up a USAID mission there. Before I left, I met with Jim Kunder, then administrator of the Agency. In those days, every USAID director met with the administrator prior to departing for the host country and new assignment, ostensibly to get his or her marching orders. My hour-plus conversation with Jim was a relaxed discussion about our respective philosophies on international development. The only marching order he gave me was to "take care of your people and the rest will follow." He was right.

Recruit and Retain the Best: Take Care of Your People

Taking care of your people begins with recruiting, then retaining, talent. The competition for talent is projected to rise in the coming decade, notwithstanding the state of the economy and the trend longevity is having on established retirement ages. Whether college recruiters, the military, or Fortune 500 companies, most organizations have shifted their focus, giving greater weight to the "softer skills." It's not that credentials don't matter; they do and always will. It's just that the distinguishing factors of success and therefore the predictive factors of success have been more finely tuned than in the past. Executives, companies, and organizations are giving more weight to applicants' abilities to continually learn and grow. How resilient are they? Can they make mistakes, learn, and adjust without crushing their self-confidence? Companies are looking for efficiency as a core value—people who make to-do lists and get things done expeditiously. They value people with a breadth of experiences that give them new insights and frames of reference. They want self-starters, people who arrive on the job with a list of things they have already accomplished through resourcefulness. Perhaps, above all, companies want the "right" player, not always the "best" player. Basically, executives and recruiters want to hire people who are comfortable in their own shoes, have big dreams, and will work extremely hard to realize those dreams.

In his book, *From Good to Great*, Jim Collins[4] claims that getting the right people "on the bus" is job number one of a great leader. The operative word there is "right." How do you define right? It can be difficult because what is right for one organization or company may not be right for another.

When John Wooden, the all-time winningest college basketball coach, talked about how he put together a team, he said he didn't always recruit the player with the best vertical jump, highest point averages, or most high school awards in the sport. This appears counterintuitive until you realize that Wooden sought out and recruited the best team players. He looked for kids who were determined and hardworking, because they fit with his philosophies and the expectations he had for his teams. He recruited self-less team players who strived for continual improvement and who contributed in intangible ways to team spirit. As an executive, you would do well to follow his example.

How do you decide who will be right for your team? First, it is important to know what you need. Ask yourself questions like these:

• What gaps am I trying to fill?

• Am I recruiting the highest GPAs?

• How do I value resiliency?

• How do I view those who have had setbacks, learned from them, and grown?

• How do I value people who have intercultural experiences, whether in their own families or by living in other countries?

• How much innovation do I want/need?

• How do I value interpersonal skills and how do I measure these?

In looking at the questions above, let's answer the one about intercultural experiences as an example. Valuing intercultural experiences is critically important in recruiting talent, because diversity in the workforce yields greater innovation, greater plurality of ideas, and more and better ways to accomplish the vision. Studies undertaken by Dr. Ruth Hill Useem at Michigan State University found that children who had lived overseas brought a wider range of ideas to problem solving than those who had not.[5] Does it matter if the person is an only child or one of a family of 15? What would each respectively bring to the job? Does it matter that a potential employee grew up in poverty versus enjoyed a privileged childhood, or did or did not face adversity of some kind? Who do you want to recruit and why? How will you measure their characteristics or skills? As an executive, you need to understand what skills you need on your team, what each staff member brings to the job, and the staff members themselves. All this you do by listening. People reveal themselves through communicating. So, listen closely, and you will recruit a great team.

Stepping Stones to Growth

Helping people grow and develop is not as easy as it sounds. Just because your team is comprised of adults doesn't mean they don't need your help. Your job is to help them get their jobs done without detailing how to do them or giving them the answers. You may know an answer to the problem and you may know how to get the result you want, but your job as an executive is to let them discover the best solution or approach to the challenge for themselves. It is counterintuitive, and it can be hard. However, when you tell people the answers, they don't learn and they don't remember. When they discover the answers for themselves, they learn. In addition, the next time they face a similar problem or situation, they will retrieve the lesson and determine if it applies to the new case. This kind of learning occurs when people have "Aha" moments, insights, or breakthroughs. As a result of these moments, their confidence is boosted, they learn, and they develop new skills and knowledge, which greatly benefits them, the team, and the organization or company.

Adults learn by experience. Experience as I discuss it here means making decisions, taking action, and making, correcting, and learning from mistakes. You need to allow the space for this to happen. It may sound like a terrible idea, but it is one of those counterintuitive actions I mentioned earlier. And, it is how adults learn, grow, and prepare for greater responsibilities.

I was fortunate enough to work for an ambassador named Lew Lucke. He understood the importance of allowing space for people to make decisions, take action, make mistakes, and learn. Once, when I divulged to him that the approach to an election administration issue in Haiti was not working and I needed to backtrack and refocus our efforts in a tactically new way, he just smiled. It was a smile that said, "I'm glad you are taking a broader look at the issue and I'm glad you have learned."

As an executive, I strived to do the same. I found it difficult to sit quietly and allow time for senior leaders to learn and grow. For example, in India when we won approval to increase our staff levels substantially, we needed space to house the new staff. We opted not to simply expand office real estate (a prohibitively expensive option). Rather, I let my executive management officer manage this project. He approached the expansion of staff like an engineer with detailed plans, lists, and projections. This is not the way I would have done it. In fact, I could have predicted the outcome, but I let him do it his way. When he began to implement the plan, he hit resistance from the staff, and he worried that all his work had been for naught. Not surprised, I guided him to take a step back, identify the issues, conduct meetings, and give people a chance to voice their concerns and offer ideas. Then, I stepped away again. He took that advice and implemented it in his own way based on his comfort level and his personally developed best practices. In the end, the executive management officer won support from the staff, the space was tailored to staff needs, creative ideas were used that weren't in his original plans, and implementation went impeccably smoothly. I can guarantee that the officer adapted, learned, and gained confidence during this exercise in leadership. In fact, he won an award for his work in India and went on to a position of greater responsibility.

As I learned in India, executives have to allow the space for others to learn. This sometimes means allowing subordinates to make mistakes, even to "fail." No one wants to talk about it, but this is how adults learn! This leadership stance, allowing mistakes and learning from them, contributes to an alluring reputation and helps with retaining talent.

No executive wants to get anywhere near failure. It is too risky. It can damage your brand. It can threaten your earning power. Superiors and the public can be quick to judge. Rest assured. You will make mistakes in your leadership role. Everyone does. Just don't make them twice. Learn from them. Ensure you have a personal or internal "learning loop" that reviews decisions made and steps taken to learn how you could have made better decisions or taken better steps. You see, you have to make mistakes in order to succeed.

Some executives and institutions may preach the "embracing failure" mantra, but they don't practice it. As soon as employees recognize this disconnect, they leave. It erodes trust and in a highly competitive environment for talent, good people will choose to go elsewhere. Executives set the tone and the standard of how much risk, error, and investment in the growth and development of their people the organization can sustain: full stop. Allowing employees space to make mistakes, learn and grow will be a differentiator in the near future.

Globally, we are beginning to see the value of resiliency. Elite colleges are picking up this idea of learning from mistakes as an important distinguisher of excellence. They are beginning to understand that as a recruiter of talent, you may not want the student with all As. Maybe you want the student who had to struggle through organic chemistry or Spanish class to succeed. Employers may want prospects who have faced adversity, did not meet expectations, but learned from the experience and gained personal insights. These people know themselves better because they have dealt with adversity. They may have resiliency skills that are crucial in the workplace and are important indicators of success.

A large part of the job of investing in staff growth and development is recruiting and retaining talent. The best way to retain talent is to create a workplace environment in which staff members can thrive, a supportive environment in which they want to work. It is a team that people want to play on because not only is it successful, but it is also fun. This type of environment attracts talent, and your job is to create such an internal environment.

Trust as the Intangible Differentiator

Establishing trust is critical to creating this ideal workplace environment. It is absolutely essential to the development of your team and to obtaining your goals of greater competitiveness and effectiveness. Many books have been written about the importance of trust building, and yet so many executives still struggle to build trust with their staff. This struggle is a testimony to how difficult it is to build trust – not just with your inner circle, the C-suite, but also with your senior leaders, managers, and employees. Note: It is your job. Trust is the foundation of great leadership and it is the key to building a strong team and having a high-performing internal environment. You are responsible for building the foundation of trust and maintaining it. You can't skip it. Everything else relies upon it. If your foundation is shaky, then everything built on top of it is also subject to instability.

So much is dependent on trust—communication, change alignment, and decisions. Great leaders not only develop a trusting relationship with their staff, they model trust as a means of helping staff grow and develop. One of the best ways to develop staff that you can trust is to earn their trust and keep it. This is far easier said than done.

Trust is easy to lose. As an executive, I was reviewing the design of an approximately $100 million South Asia regional energy program. We had had several meetings leading up to the final approval, and, with a deadline at our backs, one issue remained unresolved. It had to do with the degree to which the program should employ a political economy approach as part of policy reform. The office director, an extremely well-respected engineer who had worked in South Asia and in the energy sector his entire career, argued against such an approach. He laid out his rationale based largely on his experience. I disagreed and laid out my rationale, which was more global in nature and more broadly based in policy reform. When we couldn't reach an agreement, I declared that we were going to approach the policy reform element my way. I was the boss and it was my job to make the decision. In hindsight, this was not the best way to handle making this decision. In that moment, I lost the trust of my valued expert and colleague. I pulled the hierarchy card because I simply didn't make time to gather the information I needed to support my gut instinct. This is almost never a good idea.

Gone are the days of using positional authority over persuasive authority at the executive level. To whatever extent humanly possible, you should rely on your skills of persuasion. This doesn't mean relying on your charisma. It means calling on the trust you've built and supplementing it with convincing data and facts that lead to a firm solution or decision. If you dictate the decision and haven't persuaded the person charged with implementing it, you have, at best, an unenthusiastic soldier fighting your battles, and, at worst, a passive-aggressive operator who will gladly lead your initiative into a ditch just to be able to say, "I told you so."

Daily Deposits in the Trust Account

How do you build trust? Brené Brown, an acclaimed sociologist who studies trust and its relationship to shame and humility, says trust is built in the small moments and is related to vulnerability. She puts it like this, "We need to feel trust to be vulnerable and we need to be vulnerable in order to trust."[6] This concept is not intuitive. You may associate being vulnerable with showing weakness, but, in fact, it is a strength that leads to greater trust. Small moments, like remembering your staff members' names and those of their spouses and children, are a good starting point. Birthdays are a bonus! Remembering something intimate that a staff member has shared with you, like their dreams and ambitions, is trust-generating without a doubt. Holding in confidence personal information will build a bond. Sometimes little things like stopping by their desk to ask how their day is going will generate good feelings and build trust.

I'll give you an example of a small moment that had a big impact on me. I did not vote for Hillary Clinton in the 2008 Democratic presidential primary. I did not relate to her values, or to what I perceived as her values. Fellow Democrat Barack Obama became President and

Clinton became Secretary of State. I didn't have much of an opinion of her other than that she was smart and independent.

A few years later, I attended a State Department reception for an Indian delegation to the U.S. Secretary Clinton and President Obama both attended and each spoke briefly. The room was full of executives from both the Indian and American governments, undersecretaries of state and assistant secretaries of state, as well as my boss at the time. After the speeches and the toasts were over, everyone nestled up to the rope line to shake the dignitaries' hands. I was about four or five people deep, away from the rope, with mostly men between the rope and me. I wasn't even extending my hand for a shake. When Secretary Clinton saw me, however, she extended her hand deep into the crowd in my direction. It took me a second to realize she wanted to shake my hand. I stepped forward and extended my hand to shake hers. She had a huge smile on her face and mouthed the words "Thank you." She didn't have to do that, but her gesture completely changed my opinion of her. She built a bridge of trust by reaching out to me, woman to woman.

This is where art and science meet. By this, I mean that there is no precise recipe based on quantitative data on how to build trust. While there is a growing body of neuroscientific knowledge that relates to leadership, there is an art to building trust that is difficult, if not impossible, to quantify and measure. Building trust is, in large part, an art, because it is the result of human interactions in a dynamic environment. That said, there are some common practices that, while they don't guarantee trust, will go a long way to building it. I'll talk about these throughout the book, but here are a few common practices for getting started.

Table 2.1: Trust Builders and Busters	
Trust Builders	**Trust Busters**
Sharing information broadly	Being dishonest or deceitful, whether perceived or real
Giving credit where credit is do and even where it isn't due	Having hidden agendas or a lack of clarity of purpose
Being a team player and offering to help when you don't have to	Being greedy, taking credit when not deserved
Taking an interest in the person, before the work	Being hypercompetitive
Maintaining confidence even when not explicitly asked	Having an unrealistic image of self, showing little humility
Never disclosing intimacies shared unless permission has been explicitly granted	Expressing extreme personality preferences
Being transparent	Having clashing values
Being humble and showing humility	Breaking promises or commitments
Expressing empathy genuinely	Multitasking in front of others
Being a good listener, fully present	
Putting others first, being selfless	
Doing what you say you are going to do	

Notice that not all of these "trust busters" are malicious or intentional. Sometimes they occur when people work together and are unaware of clashes of styles, frames of reference, or personality preferences.

Measuring the Staff Development Return on Investment

If investing in, developing, and recruiting the right people, allowing for errors, and building trust are your primary job as an executive, how do you know if you are doing your job well?

If you understand that delegating decisions and responsibilities is important, and you allow space for subordinates to decide the "how" so they are empowered and allowed to grow, how long do you give people to get it right? How do you know if it is enough or too much time? This is the art of leadership. It is a judgment call. You need to know your staff well to answer these questions.

Figure 2.1 might help you answer these questions. It should be used as a rule of thumb. On the horizontal axis is time and expected due date. On the vertical axis is the quality of task and expected quality. As an executive you establish the what (quality of task) and the when (the due date or period of time to complete the task). Learning is depicted by the shaded areas. If you tell your staff members how to carry out an action, a task, a program, or how to solve the problem, the person learns relatively little and remains on the left hand side of the chart. Learning in this case is depicted by the lightest shaded area. When you allow the employee to determine the how, you can see that they will learn much more. Ideal learning is depicted by the light shaded area plus the medium shaded area – the employee learns the most while meeting the quality and time expectations. If the employee exceeds the absolute time limit and has not produced the quality "what," then return on investment in learning is diminished. The employee still learns, but your needs of quality and time have not been met.

Figure 2.1: Staff Development

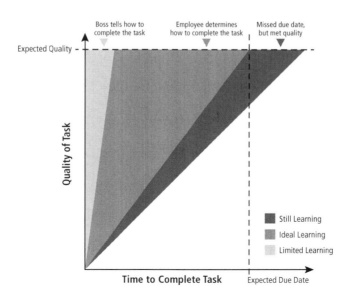

You, as the executive, monitor staff progress. If it appears that an employee needs a nudge, you can step in to offer suggestions and/or direction. You must learn through experience when to make this call.

Summary

I've touted staff growth and development as job number one of the executive, but only about 10% of your time should be spent on this aspect. This can be misleading because, in practice, everything you do contributes to the development of your staff. A part of staff growth and development is recruiting and retaining talent. This means creating a work environment that provides opportunities for growth, inculcates trust, and allows space for your people to learn from their mistakes. Another part of recruiting and retaining talent is the example you set and the behaviors you model. These attract people to your team and organization. Staff will grow tremendously in this kind of environment. You will attract and keep the right talent for your objectives, and ultimately, you will be more competitive and effective in achieving your corporate or organizational goals.

Chapter Two Secrets

1. Your number one priority is to develop your people.

2. Fail in order to succeed, but ensure the feedback loop is activated.

3. Sharpen your skills of influence. Positional authority is to be used as a last resort only. Burn the hierarchy card!

4. Get to know your staff as individuals. Listen to, understand, and learn about them.

5. Be vulnerable. Let people know that you know you don't have all the answers.

6. Build trust with your behavior. Engage staff with all your attention. Resist the temptation to multitasking in front of others.

Chapter Two Exercise

Find an executive leader you admire, introduce yourself, and meet her socially to gain her insights. Compare and contrast how you spend your time and the key components of your jobs. How does she spend her day? How is she developing people? What kinds of decisions is she making? How is she taking care of herself? How does she recruit and retain talent and take care of her people? How does she generate team spirit and how much tolerance does she have for mistakes? How does she determine the right pace and how does she explicitly build trust? Sharing this kind of information with fellow leaders serves to build your confidence.

Chapter Three

{ KEEPING UP WITH THE JONESES }

I n Chapter One, I said that 60% of an executive's time should be spent outside of the company or organization. I would go further to say that if you aren't spending this much time outside of your organization, then you aren't doing your job. I know. It seems counterintuitive. You've been hired to "run the company" or "lead the organization." It is easy to believe you should be burning the midnight oil at your office and focusing all of your time internally. However, while you should focus some of your time internally, the majority should be focused externally. This is because a significant part of your job is to develop trusting relationships with people outside of your organization who will provide useful information as you take the company forward.

What are you supposed to do out there? How should you spend your time? Well, what is your objective? Your goal is to examine the external environment to understand the outside forces that impact or could impact your organization. You will go to the proverbial mountaintop to observe all of the companies in your industry that are competing for the same market share. You will spend your time gathering information from circles of fellow executives, which is a job no one else in the organization can do for you. Then you will analyze this information and use it to improve the competitiveness of your company or the effectiveness of your organization.

So much has been written about the accelerating pace of change as a by-product of globalization and advancing technology. Many people argue that the problems we are trying to solve and the issues we are dealing with are more complex than ever before because it is tougher to distinguish cause from effect. Systems change and are more interdependent, and when combined with other variables in the environment, may create greater ambiguity about cause and effect, making it difficult to analyze a situation and predict the future. Taken together, these forces may yield problems that have many answers, but no "right" answer, just one solution that is less "bad" than the alternatives. These problems defy even complex analytical tools, and these are the types of thorny problems that are reserved for executives.

It follows that the more quality information you have about trends and new data, the more exposure to new thinking you have. The more ideas you have to bring to bear on these problems, the better able you will be to predict the future. Armed with these insights, you can shape a strategy that will result in a more competitive position for your company or a more effective organization as a whole.

One of the key aspects of an executive's job is to set the vision and develop the strategy. The more useful data, analysis, and ideas you have, the more accurately you can predict or plan for the future. You may not be able to do this with laser accuracy, but you should be able to predict a range of reasonable possibilities. Your acuity in interpreting variables and trends is heightened and your ability to "see around the corner" becomes far more accurate. Also, the more informed your strategy for improving your competitiveness or your effectiveness, the lower the calculated risk in taking a posture. This information is critical and you have to work for it. I know you thought that as an executive you were going to attend exciting cocktail receptions and host lavish dinners and it would be all fun, but these events are actually part of your workplace. It is at them that you will build stakeholder trust and gather intelligence. It is over a glass of wine or on the 18th hole that the most valuable information is often shared.

External Stakeholders

Now that you understand the importance of your time outside the organization, how do you make the most of it? First, you will want to define your external environment. The external environment is composed of those stakeholders or forces that could have an impact on your strategy and competitiveness or effectiveness or a bearing on your vision or strategy. These include institutions, people, events, and decisions outside of your company or organization. In Table 3.1, you'll find a list of external stakeholders for you to consider.

Table 3.1: External Stakeholders
Competitors (benchmarking information)
Collaborators (suppliers, overt partners, latent partners)
Board of directors
Customers and clients
Leaders of interest groups
Leaders of political organizations
Leaders of on-line communities
Captains of industry
Think tanks and policy institutes
Elected leaders (local or national)
Government leaders
Religious Leaders
Leaders of civil society (citizen, advocacy, and service groups)

After reading through this table, come up with additional external stakeholders for your particular situation. Make your own list that is as specific as possible with names of people and organizations and your rationale for including them.

External Forces

In addition to external stakeholders, there are external forces on which your attention should be focused. Some external forces that require attention and may influence your company or organization are identified in Table 3.2. Please think of forces you might add and put them on your own list.

Table 3.2: External Forces
Laws and regulations
Emerging technology
Social trends (surveys, public opinion polling)
Competition performance
World politics, political instability, risk
Innovations
Economic trends (sector, industry, regional, national, global)
Economic shocks, globalization
Immigration trends, U.S. and elsewhere
Demographic trends
Generational trends
Government policies (federal, state, local, and foreign)
Popular culture
Energy supply
Water supply
Food supply
Access to information

These are fairly macrolevel forces and it is critical that you monitor them. Keep your eye out for the occasional "curve ball," the unexpected element that could negatively impact your vision or strategy or that could create an unplanned opportunity. These are things like natural disasters or sudden shifts that are impossible or nearly impossible to anticipate.

Some examples of key documents that may prove useful in keeping abreast of these external forces are the following: Economist Intelligence Unit, Wall Street Journal, Washington Post, Huffington Post, Congressional Daily, World Economic Forum, United Nations General Assembly Reports, New York Times, Christian Science Monitor, Economist, Atlantic Monthly, Time, Newsweek, Foreign Affairs, industry-specific publications, and profession-specific publications.

Get Personal

Once you have identified external stakeholders and forces, you will want to make personal connections with your key stakeholders, who will help you understand issues, offer you their perspectives, and help you see your company or organization from an outsiders' perspective. Making these personal connections builds trust, which enables these external stakeholders to offer you valuable insights; hopefully, you can do this for them as well.

Developing trusting relationships with external stakeholders is such an important part of the executive job that much of the value you bring to the position depends on your network. The denser your network, the more potential sources you have to tap into for information and perspectives, the more valuable you will be to your organization or company. If you have ever wondered why ascending officers should network, or why 60% of an executive's time should be spent outside the organization, now you know. It's to build these networks and to gather information that is critical to the success of the company or organization.

Not Just Any Information

When you are ready to proceed with gathering and analyzing information that is useful, it is important to first identify the type of information you need, why you need it, and which of your sources are most reliable and credible relative to what you need. Here are the steps:

1. Start by identifying the kinds of information that could be useful in reducing uncertainty.

2. Next, identify the kinds of information that could pose a threat to your strategy.

3. Finally, identify the kinds of information that could pose an opportunity for your strategy.

You will want to hone in on this information because reducing uncertainty and threats and increasing opportunities will ultimately increase the likelihood of success.

Triage!

You'll want to stay abreast of issues and opportunities as they arise, but there's a challenge to information gathering. Especially in large companies and organizations, this kind of information is probably gathered and managed by experts in their technical field. As an executive, you will constantly receive this information, but it is too much! So, you must triage it, i.e., organize it into categories for you and your company or organization's consumption. Some information you want regularly, and some daily or weekly. Collect it only as often as you will use it. Some of this information you will want to gather continuously as it is reported daily or weekly. Some you will want less frequently, but still regularly, e.g., quarterly, semiannually, or annually, because it shines a light on progress, trends, and lessons learned. This type of regular reporting can delineate issues and offer course corrections. It also includes macroenvironmental trends and a check on assumptions in your strategy to determine whether they are still valid. Other kinds of information may be event-driven, as in the case of a crisis or unexpected shock to the system. A natural disaster can disrupt, for example, supply chains. Changes in political administrations can dramatically change policy. These kinds of events and information are usually reactive in nature and may or may not impact your strategy.

The point is, as the executive, you will be inundated with information and reports, both external and that generated internally. You need to prioritize all of this information based on the vision, goals, and strategy of your organization or company. Of all the reports, which ones will you pay the most attention to? Which ones will you expect your senior team to digest? You will determine over time and through discussions with your external stakeholders and senior team which information is most valuable. Once you decide what is most valuable to your external assessment, convey it to your senior team. This is a good way for them to learn what is important to you. Also, let them know what your expectations are in terms of their external assessments. This will be indispensable because, as senior leaders, they will conduct their own external assessments of their targeted stakeholders and their specific needs, which will differ from yours.

Information Is the New Natural Resource

With the technological advancements of the 21st century, companies and organizations that can master the collection, synthesis, and use of new data have a competitive edge over those that cannot. In many ways, information is like a new natural resource.

Depending on the size of your company or organization, you may have a whole army of people who do a lot of information gathering, analyzing, collating, and reporting for you. Your job is to "ground truth" the conclusions of that information in your circles and from your executive perspective. If you are, figuratively speaking, "above" others, you should have a broader perspective, be able to see further into the distance, and use your information to predict likely future scenarios. This allows you to develop a strategy or adjust a strategy to weather the threats and take full advantage of the future landscape and the emerging opportunities presented in your predicted scenario. Clearly, the better your information is, the better your analysis will be, and the clearer and more accurate your predicted scenario or range of scenarios will be. A strategy built on an accurate projection of the future is a strategy set to succeed.

Avoid the Obvious

One very important "watch out for" tip is to be extremely careful to avoid confirmation bias, a term from organizational psychology that refers to paying selective attention to data or input that confirms your predicted scenario and ignoring data or input that contradicts it. It is like selective hearing. You pick up on data that are consistent with your ideas, theories, and hypotheses and conveniently (though subconsciously) ignore those that are inconsistent. As an executive who operates in a high-stakes arena, falling prey to confirmation bias can be disastrous for you and your company or organization. Avoid it at all costs.

Avoid Surprises

A stark example of the difference a good external assessment can make to your strategy is what happened during the terrorist attacks of 9/11. The United States was a nation in shock. Why? Our leaders had not spent the time and effort to conduct a good external analysis. We know in hindsight that important information wasn't gathered, analyzed, and synthesized. Our leaders didn't have an accurate picture of the future or the range of possible futures, and our national security strategy was not informed with an accurate external assessment. The 9/11 commissioners stated as much in their report.[7]

"The most important failure was one of imagination. We do not believe leaders understood the gravity of the threat. The terrorist danger from Bin

Ladin and al Qaeda was not a major topic for policy debate among the public,
the media, or in the Congress…

"The missed opportunities to thwart the 9/11 plot were also symptoms
of a broader inability to adapt the way government manages problems to the
new challenges of the twenty-first century…

"There were broader management issues with respect to how top leaders
set priorities and allocated resources…

"The U.S. government did not find a way of pooling intelligence and
using it to guide the planning and assignment of responsibilities for joint
operations involving entities as disparate as the CIA, the FBI, the State De-
partment, the military, and the agencies involved in homeland security."

For the intelligence community, bureaucratic rivalries contributed, in part, to the lack of a sharing of information. Competition among
agencies and other parts of the government for resources, attention, and
credibility was partly to blame for the lack of foresight. The information
these agencies gathered individually was of limited use, but when pieced
together could have painted a clearer picture of the future. This "view
around the corner" could have altered our imaginations and, in turn,
impacted our national security strategy to better protect the country.

Indeed, a key element in the 9/11 Commission's recommendations to enhance national security is to unify strategic intelligence with
a new National Intelligence Director and a National Counterterrorism
Center. The idea is to systematically pull together the knowledge outside
of individual government organizations and allow critical information
flows that transcend agency boundaries and rivalries.

The private sector is somewhat different from government entities,
because although government departments are in some sense "competing" against each other for a share of scarce resources, they aren't
competing for a share of the market like companies in the private sector.
Within an industry, information and knowledge are key to a company's
ability to adapt and compete.

Sleeping with the Enemy

It may seem counterintuitive, but the solutions to your problems as an executive leader may rest with your peers. You are not going to discover these answers or solutions without conveying your challenges to them. You may not want to give away all your secrets to your fiercest competitors, but in sharing information with peer companies, you may be surprised at what you will discover. Perhaps your peer's company has faced a similar problem and used an approach that would benefit your company. Perhaps that particular approach won't work, but you may be able to build on it to develop a novel, tailored approach for your own company. Perhaps you will gain new insights from different perspectives. Perhaps you will have that "light bulb" moment when you synthesize several bits of information to yield a breakthrough idea, approach, or product. Nate Collins, former president and chairman of the board of BancTexas, recollects when, prior to banking deregulation, chief credit officers cooperated to help each other solve problems. This kind of network of quasi-competitors was organized by the banking industry's Robert Morris Association, a network consisting of the top 25 chief credit officers in the nation. Nate was part of this group of his peers. When he had trouble getting his president and chairman of the board to understand the value of checks and balances between the volume and quality of loans, he called on his counterparts at the Bank of America, the Bank of Detroit, and the largest bank in Florida to convince his leadership of the value. In this case, cooperation with these quasi-competitors helped ensure the longer-term financial sustainability of BancTexas.[8]

Innovation is the fuel of competition and companies are finding value in sharing information, research results, issues, lessons, and technologies with peers as a means of creating new products, services, and ways of doing business. For example, nearly 50 years ago in Japan, Nippon Telephone and Telegraph, Nippon Sheet Glass, and Sumitomo Electric Industries fused their respective technologies—cable, glass, and electronics—to produce fiber optics. This is, in part, why the Japanese hold a significant share of the global market in this product today.[9]

Crossing industries and engaging peers who aren't direct competitors can be a less risky way of sharing information and seeking solutions. It may lead to a cooperative relationship that over time produces business alliances with unlikely partners outside of your industry. This is what happened when Sharp combined crystal technology with optics and electronic technologies to produce liquid crystal displays (LCDs). These displays are now used in calculators and this technology was leveraged into more than a third of the global market for LCDs.[10]

In India right now there are dozens of companies chasing the secret to building and maintaining a distribution network for a population of 1.2 billion (and growing) people. Everyone sees the value in it, but the sheer size, diversity, and varied state of development in India belie traditional or standard approaches. However, these companies are not sharing information with each other about the lessons they've learned with their various approaches. The solution, in all likelihood, lies within these competitors. This is a clear case where cooperation would trump competition and the solution(s) would be greater than the sum of the parts. However, it would require businesses to share secrets with each other. This counterintuitive act requires levels of trust one can only build by developing relationships with external actors, even competitors.

Summary

Now that you understand the number and variety of external stakeholders with which you must interact, you are beginning to get a clearer understanding of how this can easily take 60% or more of your time. You can also understand how important trust is to learning information, sharing perspectives, and reciprocating data and advice. You can see how, as an executive, you must explore latent alliances and remain open to the possibility of learning from those from whom you may not expect to learn. Information gathered from external sources and through an examination of external forces feed your strategy, and your strategy, in large part, determines your success.

Chapter Three Secrets

1. Collaboration is more advantageous to obtaining information from stakeholders than competition.

2. Great executives know their key stakeholders and why they are critical to achieving their vision.

3. Seek to understand external forces with an eye toward the potential "curve ball."

4. Manage the information: don't let it manage you!

5. Elite executives guard against confirmation bias when interpreting or analyzing data.

6. An executive's effectiveness is a function of her interpersonal relationships.

Chapter Three Exercise

Map out all of the external stakeholders and forces important to your strategy. Identify contacts for each and schedule time to meet with each one at least once a year, or more frequently as warranted. For those external stakeholders or forces without a contact, identify how you can make contact to obtain the needed information.

Chapter Four

{ # ALL SYSTEMS GO! }

While executives spend 60% of their time focused externally, developing relationships and gathering information and perspectives, they spend the remaining time focused internally. As an executive, once you have gathered, analyzed, and synthesized information from external sources and forces for input into your vision and strategy, you must then devote time to gathering, analyzing, and synthesizing information from inside the company for the same purpose. All of this information will be combined to produce the vision, goal, and strategy for the company or the organization.

First, a warning: Many executives spend too much time focused internally. Why? Sometimes, the executive is not completely clear on what he should and should not pay attention to internally. He falls into the trap of jumping the walls of his primary responsibilities back to responsibilities he had before his executive position. He gets caught in a never-ending list of decisions or actions that fall outside of his core executive responsibility. These time-consuming functions consume the executive's energy and limit his ability to focus on his key responsibilities such that he isn't able to spend the time he should focused on external stakeholders and forces, for example.

So let's look at what executives should and should not focus on internally. One of your key responsibilities is to ensure that all the internal systems that make your company or organization function are aligned behind the vision and strategy and that they are consistent with the core values that have been established. All internal systems need to ensure that the structure suits or supports the goals and objectives of the strategy. The most important areas to focus on when conducting internal assessments are the vision and strategy, the structure, and leadership consistency.

Vision and Strategy

After you have developed your vision and strategy, be crystal clear in communicating it. Highlight a few key strategic priorities. Know how you will earn or maintain your competitive advantage. Ask yourself, what will your company be known for? Will your company be a leader in a technical field or the best at customer service? Will it be known as an innovator or for providing the lowest cost for value? Will it be known for producing products that fuse technologies or perfecting energy-efficient processes? The qualities that distinguish your organization or company must be the key components of your strategy. They will guide your internal assessment because, ideally, you want every system and every person focused on those elements of your strategy that make you effective or competitive. Vision and strategy are discussed in more detail in Chapter Five.

Structure

The structure is how a company is organized to carry out its strategy and achieve results. There is no single best way to organize, because every company's strategy, priorities, and assets vary tremendously, and the structure is a reflection of those variables. The structure is how authority is distributed and the rationale behind that distribution. It is reporting lines and the extent to which staff work together to achieve results.

While there is no single best way to structure your organization or company, I would offer this: Ensure that checks and balances are established between and among systems. You don't want too much power or authority to rest in any one place. The most functional workplaces are those in which neither the CFO, COO, nor CEO has complete authority. For any one position to have complete authority is unhealthy, and ultimately, high risk. You want both interdependency and checks and balances.

Next, you want to be sure that the established processes for interaction among and between substructures or subunits are lean and efficient. Some organizations structure themselves functionally, with, for example, product designers, manufacturers, and marketers operating separately. Some companies or organizations operate using a hierarchical structure, which, assuming it supports your strategy, has advantages. Some operate using a matrix management or cross-functional structure. This also has distinct advantages, but can produce conflict if levels of trust aren't high. The point is that the structure needs to fit the strategy. If your strategy has complex, ambitious goals and your company prides itself on teamwork, your structure needs to reflect that, as do all the other systems that support your strategy.

Once you have the structure and have determined that it supports the vision, strategy, and key priorities, turn to how these structural elements interact. Every organization must have some bureaucratic processes; however, when you are evaluating alignment, you are checking to ensure these are, in fact, value-added processes and not entrenched, power-wielding, or unnecessary steps. It is distressing, but all too common, to see staff members who have been in a company or organization for a decade or more insert unnecessary processes, procedures, or steps that ultimately slow down your processes and create inefficiencies that render your company less competitive or your organization less effective.

Leadership Consistency

Finally, and most importantly, as part of an internal assessment, it is important to look at the top managers: the executive team. You want to ensure that leadership is consistent with the intrinsic values of the organization or the company.

Institutions have shared intrinsic values, intangible qualities that give meaning to the day-to-day work for most people in the organization or the company. They drive the workforce. Sometimes these values are ideas, or ideals. Sometimes they are the vision itself. In my line of work, international development, the workforce at USAID shared a belief in the mission of eliminating poverty worldwide. USAID employees are an extremely passionate group. Any leader who indicated, in any way, shape, or form, that he didn't share the value of helping to genuinely make the world a better place immediately lost credibility.

Leaders' values are constantly on display in what and how they communicate, in how they act, and with whom they interact. Staff members look for this consistency in values and reward it with their trust. As an executive, more than perhaps any other employee, your espoused values must be consistent or aligned with those of your company or organization, as well as with your own actions. When the values of an executive are out of alignment, trust erodes quickly. All of the elements needed for leaders to be successful and achieve their goals—relationship building, influencing staff members to follow you, communicating, driving change, gathering critical information from within the organization—are based on trust. So having alignment of values (the foundation of trust) is an absolute must.

The newspapers are full of reports about executive leaders, from CEOs and presidents to generals and elected officials, whose behavior was inconsistent with both their espoused values and the values of the institutions they were leading. This leaves a mark on the leader as well as on the organization that he or she led. It is very difficult for an individual and/or institution to regain the trust of stakeholders, employees, and the public once they have been marked as inconsistent with their values.

Systems Aligned

Ensuring the alignment of internal systems is an executive's responsibility. Within an organization or company, all kinds of systems exist. They may be called by different names, but essentially, systems are put in place to help achieve the goals and objectives of the vision and strategy. In order to best support the vision and strategy, these systems must be aligned with each other. Here are the kinds of systems common to most institutions:

- *Personnel system:* This includes how employees are recruited, hired, removed, promoted, and rewarded. It also includes skills that set your organization apart, how people are nurtured for growth, and training and coaching programs.

- *Decision-making systems:* Encompass how decisions about resources, planning, and budgeting are made.

- *Culture and values:* These are genuinely shared by staff and socialized into new employees to create and maintain the desired environment in the organization or company. (This will be discussed in detail in Chapter Seven.)

- *Learning system:* As well as the knowledge management system for culling lessons learned, sharing them with the workforce, and adjusting other systems accordingly.

Incongruent Values

   If it is so important to have value alignment, how does it happen that leaders fall so far off the beam? There are many theories out there. My theory is that as an executive, it is easy to confuse the position you hold with the person you are. You spend much time both during and outside of regular office hours interacting with people as an executive. When you are in the executive position, you have handlers who restrict access and also sometimes information; you are in a bubble of sorts. Everyone, it seems, wants time with you. You begin to think it is you they want to see. In fact, nine times out of ten, it is the position you hold in which they are interested, not you. Separate yourself from your position. When you are asked to make speeches and do interviews, keep in mind that, in all likelihood, it is your position and title that they are interested in, not you. If John Doe held the same position, they would want time with him. If you lose this perspective, your thinking will become distorted and trouble will start. The lesson here is to know your values, be sure they are aligned with those of your company or organization, and check in with yourself periodically to ensure that your behavior is consistent with your stated values.

The more aligned these systems are with each other and to the vision and strategy, the more efficiently and effectively the organization or company will operate. Think of your organization or company like a human body with its digestive, lymphatic, cardiovascular, and reproductive systems. When all of the body's systems are aligned, the body works well. You feel good, and you are healthy. When one system stops functioning properly, you don't feel right. Because these bodily systems are interdependent, when something goes wrong with one system it often affects another.

Institutions are similar in that the finance, personnel, policy, and strategy systems are interrelated. A change in one system, for better or worse, can affect a change in another system. When things are not working properly or effectively, leaders often turn to organizational or business "doctors" like leadership and business coaches, organizational development experts, or other leaders who have had experience dealing with similar issues. All these experts do the same thing a medical doctor would do with a sick patient. They diagnose the malfunction or "illness" and issue a set of prescribed steps to take to improve the functionality of the system.

One can see the power of systems alignment through an example from my past. In college at the University of Wisconsin, I was on the rowing crew. Rowing is a sport of ultimate and pure alignment. To win a race on the water, each team member must know her strength and that of her teammates. The coxswain, who sits at the rear of the boat, yells guidance to individual rowers to ensure that each is rowing in unison. And when I say unison, I mean, precisely and perfectly the same, despite the multiples of variables (height and weight of individual rowers, proportion of body parts, legs and arms and trunk, strength, rhythm, wind speed, and accuracy of coxswain).There are hundreds of different data points to consider and manage. The timing of the entry of the oar into the water, the depth in the water the oar travels, the angle of insertion and removal of the oar from the water on each stroke, the speed of movement of each rower's body in the boat, the precise angles of the head, shoulders, and so on, all contribute to the speed of the boat through the water. Measurements were taken daily on multiples of these variables. The aim was perfect alignment. While rarely obtained, when we achieved it, it felt divine. It felt effortless and it felt like we were winners.

Misalignments Are the Executive's Problem

Misalignments are quite common, and they feel something like driving on square wheels. The ride is rough at best. In some cases, the organization can't go anywhere. The square wheels manifest as staff without appropriate or needed skills; a leader whose style is inconsistent with values; or a strategy that is out of line with the corporate culture. You can see it in a lack of communication, consistently long hours, and staff whose lives are out of balance, stressed, and unhealthy. It may seem counterintuitive, but these are the executive's problems. These are indicators of system misalignments. These misalignments in the workplace spill over and affect the alignment—and ultimately, the physical and mental health—of employees.

So what do you do? It is your responsibility to ensure alignment. Review the data. It will indicate which system is out of line. For example, if the data show that 90% of employees are receiving outstanding performance ratings, but quarterly targets are consistently being missed, then perhaps the personnel system isn't supporting the strategy. If targets are being met and exceeded, but you don't know why, then look to the learning system to capture why. If policy is being made, but employees aren't following it, then there is clearly misalignment, perhaps with the culture or personnel reward system. If employees are being trained in supervisory skills, but the skill is being adopted by only 10% of new supervisors, as reflected in internal surveying, then perhaps the personnel system of incentives and rewards isn't supporting the use of that new skill or the leader doesn't give it enough import. This will be reflected in his own paucity of skill use or promotion of high potentials who don't exhibit strong supervisory skills. These are just a few examples of how systems are interdependent and how both quantitative and qualitative data can give you insights into misalignments.

Once the misalignment is diagnosed, you can make decisions— staffing, budgetary, or policy—to bring the system into better alignment. You can understand how this is an iterative process that over time brings the company or organization closer to complete alignment. You get the data from the systems themselves, especially the learning system, because it can play a catalytic role in improving the alignment of all systems within the company or organization. First though, let's look at the personnel system. Then we'll delve into the decision-making and learning systems.

Personnel System

The personnel system is responsible for the recruitment, selection, hiring, induction, evaluation, and separation of employees, as well as for incentives, rewards, and promotions. Incentives and rewards are strong shapers of behavior. Pay close attention to them. If you have a strategy that can only be achieved with teamwork, yet the meaningful rewards are given to individuals, then this is a serious disconnect. If you need to recruit staff members who are innovators, but you send a recruiter who doesn't mirror that innovative spirit, you may have the reason for your inability to recruit the kind of people you want to hire. A competitive promotion system could be undermining the matrix management structure needed to produce new products. These are the kinds of disconnects to look for in your assessment.

The personnel system should be able to produce a wealth of data for your assessment. Are you hiring the right people with the needed skills and experiences? If not, where and how are you recruiting? Do the demographics and prior experiences reflect the kinds of diversity of experience you need to carry out your strategy? Are you losing good candidates in the selection process? Does your salary and benefits package reflect market demands? Are new employees introduced to the company in the most advantageous way? Do they understand the strategy and where they fit in its achievement? Do they understand the culture? Are expectations clear? What are your retention rates? What is the success rate of annual performance evaluations and do they accurately distinguish high performers? These are the kinds of questions to ask to determine if the personnel system is aligned and supportive of the organization's vision and strategy.

Decision-Making System

The decision-making system is simply how the company or organization makes decisions. This system reflects the company's structure and values. If aligned, it supports the strategy and engages staff appropriately in decisions that affect them and their units, subgoals, and subobjectives. This system or process for making decisions can affect almost every other part of the institution. Within this system, decisions are made that affect planning and resource allocation, including staff and funding, as well as policies that guide the entire institution.

When examining the decision-making system, the executive should focus on answering such questions as: How are decisions made? What is the degree of transparency? And, what is the degree of delegation? For example, you want to know which decisions are made at the executive level and which are delegated to line officers. It is important to know how much discretion is left to individuals in decision making and how much is done as a group. Are decisions made as a consensus, by the most senior person, or by a self-selected group? Does how the decision is made depend on the decision itself and what is at stake?

Two rules of thumb come in handy here. First, you want to delegate as much as you can to the lowest level as is feasible to make decisions. This promotes empowerment and engagement and also engenders trust. Second, you want to reserve the most complex, highest risks decisions for your executive group. These are the kinds of decision that affect the entire enterprise and/or can make or break your strategy. There is a second tier of decisions that you will want to be consulted on and you may even reserve a "veto power" regarding such decisions. Routine decisions should be handled by the decision-making system, the delegated authority, the structure in place, and so on. All should support the vision and strategy. As with your executive decisions, you will want to ensure that all nonroutine decisions are made with sufficient debate and diversity of viewpoints to keep the system sharp. Consider alternatives adequately, and ultimately this will produce the best decisions. Decision-making systems will be discussed in greater detail in Chapter Nine.

Learning System

The learning system is a "system of systems." All organizations should have a feedback loop that functions as a way to compare intended impact or progress against actual gains and dissect actual performance for lessons to be fed back into the system and inculcated throughout the organization. The learning system is designed to assist an organization in collecting, analyzing, and learning from information systematically. While most organizations and companies have this system, it may not function in a way that actually supports learning. An environment that supports and values learning serves as the engine to achieving enduring results or effectiveness.

How do you know if your company or organization's learning system is at peak performance? Table 4.1 reveals some indicators of thriving learning systems, as well as some signs of handicapped learning systems, i.e., those in which the system and the supporting environment may not be aligned with the larger vision, goals, or strategy.

Table 4.1: Indicators of Learning Systems	
Peak-Performing Learning System	**Handicapped Learning System**
At regular intervals, information is collected and analyzed. Conclusions are fed back into the system for organization or company-wide learning.	Information is hoarded and not offered up to the system so that others can learn from it.
Employees at all levels feel safe in disagreeing and asking challenging questions.	The learning system is marginalized, often by separating it functionally or structurally from other systems.
People are allowed to admit they are wrong without negative consequences.	The learning system is understaffed.
Mistakes are viewed as opportunities to learn and are not cloaked in secrecy.	The lessons derived or the conclusions drawn to improve the organization or company are simply not used or acted upon.
Risk of experimentation is low enough to allow for failure and to learn from it.	There is an environment of individual accountability in which the risk of innovation or experimentation is so high that people avoid it.
The organization or company contributes to advancing the body of knowledge in its industry or arena.	Time is not taken or given to think, to examine and reexamine the big questions facing the company or organization.
New employees are briefed on the system and encouraged to use it.	No executive within the organization or company is charged with leading the learning system.
Employees are given time for reflection to think about issues, new information, and insights.	

As an executive leader, it is your job to create the type of environment that invites learning. To do this, you must engage in the learning system as a means of showing support for the system. Use it during annual reviews to generate new knowledge and to train employees. Feed tough questions into the system and allow it to generate answers for you. Check periodically to ensure that information and lessons are being collected and shared across the organization. Challenge the system by giving it future scenarios and note how it suggests that the company respond. Ensure that people have time to absorb these lessons. The executive leader's reliance on and support of the learning system will invite others to follow suit and enhance its esteem and effectiveness.

Conducting an Internal Assessment

Sometimes the job of internal assessment is so big that executives either have in-house experts do it or engage outsiders to help produce a quality assessment that helps the organization move from strategy to change agenda to internal alignment. Experts, in-house or external, use any number of analytical tools to assess data and uncover misalignments. Information from the assessment of the external environment is combined with results of an internal assessment to further refine the strategy. Many tools exist to help guide you through these steps, analysis, and thinking. Examples of strategy development tools are SWOT analysis[11], Porter's Five Forces[12,13], and Kaplan's Balanced Scorecard.[14] These tools will be discussed in greater detail in Chapter Five. There are tools for analyzing the extent of your alignment—how well your internal systems are supporting your vision and strategy—and you may already have one that your company or organization uses with great facility. The important point is to choose one that you are comfortable with and use it.

While you are conducting, digesting, and reflecting on the results of the external and internal assessments, it is essential to face facts. Be realistic about the change agenda that must be pursued in order for the company or organization to succeed.

Strategy and Change Agenda

The product of the application of the strategy development tool, with inputs from the external environment information and analysis along with internal information and data from systems and analysis of alignment, becomes the strategy. The gap between where you are today and where you want to be as a company or organization (your vision and goal) is the change agenda. The strategy is how you will close this gap.

The change agenda is the path to greater alignment and strategy implementation and consists of the prescribed actions or steps you will take for greater alignment. Keep in mind that change tends to take longer than you will expect, so be realistic in setting time frames for change initiatives. The strategy and change agenda are such important parts of the executive leader's job that Chapters Five and Six are devoted to a fuller explanation.

Summary

Remember, to be a great executive leader you need to know what your job is and how to carry it out. A significant amount of your time will be focused on internal systems and ensuring that the checks and balances are in place, the internal processes are lean and efficient, and the systems are in alignment with the larger vision, goal, and strategy.

Chapter Four Secrets

1. Data, analysis, and trends predict future scenarios or a range of potential scenarios.

2. Better data lowers risk.

3. Checks and balances among systems are well-established as a way to lower your risk.

4. Bureaucratic processes must be value added—nothing more, nothing less.
5. Internal alignment begins with the executive's values and how consistent these are with the company's or organization's values.

6. Attaining perfect alignment of internal systems requires perseverance in collecting data, learning from it, and adjusting resources and policies.

Chapter Four Exercise

Conduct a systems checkup. Make a list of all the data sources you routinely receive and the corresponding system that produces it. Ask yourself what important information you are missing. Check if the systems are interdependent. Check if you are getting data from the system that is indicators of success or progress. Check if data provided indicates missed targets or misalignments. Take corrective action, as appropriate.

Chapter Five

{ DRAW THE MAP }

In this chapter we are going to discuss creating the vision and strategy for your organization or company. Let's start with what we know. Following are some examples of good and not-so-good vision statements from some real-world companies. Review them and think about which ones appeal to you and why.

• *Alcoa:* Our vision is to be the best company in the world—in the eyes of our customers, shareholders, communities, and people. We expect and demand the best we have to offer by always keeping Alcoa's values top of mind.

• *Anheuser-Busch:* Be the world's beer company. Through all of our products, services, and relationships, we will add to life's enjoyment.

- *Avon:* To be the company that best understands and satisfies the product, service, and self-fulfillment needs of women—globally.

- *Chevron:* At the heart of The Chevron Way is our vision…to be the global energy company most admired for its people, partnership, and performance.

- *Epson:* Epson is committed to the relentlessness pursuit of innovation in compact, energy-saving, high-precision technologies, and through the formation of group-wide platforms will become a community of robust businesses, creating, producing, and providing products and services that emotionally engage customers worldwide.

- *Heinz:* To be the world's premier food company, offering nutritious, superior-tasting foods to people everywhere.

- *Ken Blanchard Companies:* To be the number one advocate in the world for human worth in organizations.

- *Kraft:* Helping People Around the World Eat and Live Better.

- *McDonalds:* Our customers' favorite place and way to eat.

- *Nike:* To be the number one athletic company in the world.

- *Qualcomm:* To deliver the world's most innovative wireless solutions.

- *Sears:* To be the preferred and most trusted resource for the products and services that enhance home and family life.

- *Walmart:* Saving people money to help them live better.

- *Zappos:* One day, 30% of all retail transactions in the U.S. will be online. People will buy from the company with the best service and the best selection. Zappos.com will be that online store.

Hold onto your thoughts about these vision statements while we review what makes a great vision statement in the next few pages.

Developing the vision statement and the strategy to carry it out is one of your key responsibilities as an executive. However, somewhat counterintuitively, you should never develop the vision by yourself. Even if a leader is brilliant and visionary, the vision should be a shared vision. There is no better way to achieve a shared vision than to have others within the organization or company help to develop it. The development processes contribute to a broader understanding and buy-in of the vision. It's not that a visionary leader can't come up with the vision herself; it's simply that it is much more powerful if the people who have a stake in fulfilling it help develop it.

For example, for four years I served in an office charged with helping others in the enterprise develop unit strategies. The most common problems I saw were no different than the problems commonly seen in the private sector or in other government institutions. Often, the vision and strategy were simply not there, or if they were there, they weren't clear to everyone. It was common to simply see a list of objectives or statement of principles and some general lofty notion of an ideal future. This isn't a strategy.

If a statement of strategy does exist, a common problem is that the strategy isn't clearly articulated. The strategy is the document of the "how," e.g., how a company intends to gain or maintain competitive advantage or market share. It is how an organization intends to fulfill its mission. It is the reason that the company exists. It explains how resources (money, people, time, energy, emotions) will be used to obtain the vision and ultimate goals described in the strategy. Often, you find the strategy sitting on a shelf in the executive's office or reduced to bullets in a presentation for outsiders.

One telltale sign of alignment and ownership of the strategy is to ask employees at various levels of the company to articulate it and cite what their part is in carrying it out. It is especially telling if you ask the maintenance staff, new employees, or those at the edge of the enterprise, furthest away from the C-suite, these questions. When entry-level staff members can articulate the vision and know their role in carrying out the strategy, their part in achieving that vision, it is a sign of a strong, well-led organization.

Oftentimes, you'll find an organization that has a vision and a strategy and staff who know what these are, but they don't buy into it. They don't understand the decisions and the trade-offs made in the decision-making process. In some cases, they outright disagree with the approach. It does little good for staff to know the strategy if they don't support it.

Having a vision developed from within the company or organization and a well-articulated strategy that people understand and can repeat back to you is important. But when all staff members, from top to bottom, know the strategy and their roles in it and also understand and believe in that strategy, it's a good indicator of a well-led outfit. How would your company or organization measure up against this indicator?

If You Don't Know Where You Are Going, Any Route Will Take You There!

You might ask yourself, what is a vision? If we don't have one, how do we get one? A vision is a picture of a future that doesn't currently exist. It is intended to motivate people. It needs to hit a "sweet spot" of inspiration—be ambitious enough to inspire people but not so ambitious that it isn't believable. If it is too ambitious, if the bar is set too high, then somewhat counterintuitively, it loses its motivating qualities. So, while you want to "dream the impossible dream," you also want to create a vision that staff and others can picture and believe possible. Your vision or ultimate goal should be out of reach in the short-term and just out of reach in the long-term.

Vision is a statement of a future state, 10 or 20 years in the future. It is the driving force behind the organization. It is the reason the company exists. It is backed by rationale and analysis from the external environment assessment, combined with an honest internal assessment of the organization's strengths and opportunities. It is accompanied by pictures and should evoke a feeling. Technically, a vision should be a brief statement that is simple and straightforward. Many companies' vision statements are expressed as a tagline, like some of the most famous, Microsoft's "A computer on every desk," Coca-Cola's "Refresh the world's consumers," and Stanford University's "Become the Harvard of the West."

A vision is a simple, direct statement of the end state of your organization or company—10 or 20 years out at a minimum. It is concise; just a sentence will do. It creates a picture or idea in the minds of those who read or hear it. It should be something everyone from the janitor to your mother can remember and repeat with ease. It is not a branding tagline, but people often confuse the two, especially when the tagline is a shortened version of the vision statement. For example, McDavid, a leader in sports-oriented medical and protective products, has a vision "to be an essential part of every athlete's training, motivation, and success."[15] But the McDavid tagline of "First on, last off" is intended to attract hardworking athletes who believe in themselves. The vision and tagline are clearly different. Other companies don't have such a clear distinction. Remember, a vision captures the future you are trying to create. It should energize, motivate, and perhaps convey a standard of excellence.

Go back and look over the vision statements at the beginning of this chapter. How do they hold up against these standards? Which are the best? What is your company or organization's vision? How does it measure up with the ones listed? Does it hit the "sweet spot"?

Technically, the executive leader is responsible for setting the vision. This is something that cannot and should not be delegated. It is the head and heart of an organization. Ostensibly, the executive is best positioned to see the future and extrapolate trend lines that feed into setting the vision. Executives should have a good sense of the resources needed to fulfill a vision. Ideally, establishing a vision is done with, at a very minimum, the senior team, the C-suite, or the top tier. Usually, the board of directors will give guidance as well. In the public sector, the President of the United States will lay out a grand vision from his party's political platform and the policies he or she (maybe in the future) establishes and was elected to pursue. In today's world, with all the information-gathering technology tools for gaining input, there is no reason to establish a vision from behind closed doors. In fact, it is counterproductive to decree a vision without the input of staff and employee engagement.

Strategy: How Will You Get There?

Once you've done the analysis, reflection, and employee engagement to establish the vision, the strategy should be relatively logical, but it isn't always. What is a strategy? Strategy is the plan for attaining and maintaining advantage over competitors. It is the broad plan, the "how," for achieving the vision and goals. Simply put, the strategy is the game plan you use to win or reach your goal. It begins with an explicitly stated assumption about the future. From there, it moves into how the institution will combine strengths and opportunities to minimize weaknesses and address threats.

There are many tools and methods for arriving at your strategy. They all involve a similar kind of analysis. Some are higher risk because they force you to predict a future with a high degree of accuracy. Others allow you to predict a range of possible futures and broaden an array of strategic choices within those presumed futures.

Here are three commonly used tools for developing a strategy:

1. A simple Strengths, Weaknesses, Opportunities, and Threats (SWOT) analysis.[16] Made popular by Albert Humphrey in the 1960s, it is still used today by many strategy developers. The SWOT aims to align the internal environment with the external environment and capitalize on specific strengths of the company or organization and position it to take advantage of opportunities. A SWOT analysis can be applied to the institution as a whole individual systems or sub-systems, as necessary.

2. A Five Forces analysis.[17] Developed by Michael Porter, this comprehensive analysis looks at competitors, bargaining power of buyers and suppliers, threats of new entrants into the market, and threats of alternative products or services. By understanding these five forces, you can strategically position your company to take advantage of emerging trends and minimize constraints that could negatively impact your competitiveness.

3. Kaplan's Balanced Scorecard.[18] This can be used not only to conduct the analysis needed to articulate the strategy, but also to put in place a system for planning and measuring strategy progress. This tool focuses on ensuring that systems within the organization are aligned with the strategy, and it captures a broader number of indicators of progress, similar to a "dashboard" of indicators.

How Do You Develop a Strategy?

Regardless of which analytical tool you use, the strategy emerges from analysis and is filtered through a series of decisions that aim to achieve or maintain competitive advantage and/or organizational effectiveness. Ideally, a strategy takes advantage of your organization's strengths and opportunities while mitigating threats to achieving its goals and objectives. The following examples will help explain this further.

While at USAID, I led a $500 million program in Peru aimed at reducing the production of coca, the leaf used in making cocaine. The program focused on the geographic regions of the country conducive to growing the coca plant. As a new leader, one of the first things I did was to understand the competition. In this case, it was the narco-traffickers, who purchased the coca leaves from poor farmers. Gathering data on these narco-traffickers proved quite difficult, but I was able to determine that they were a relatively small group with only a handful of spokespeople. Their strength was seemingly endless amounts of money, which enabled them to move fast. They operated clandestinely, far away from the cities, in rural towns where there was little state presence at all. They paid the coca farmers small sums and intimidated them with violence.

Looking at our strengths, we had the law and people's desire for peace and security on our side. We hadn't leveraged the media yet. We hadn't given the poor farmers a viable alternative. We had the national government and (at least publicly) the locally elected mayors on our side. This meant that the provision of public services was something that could be used. We hadn't engaged politicians and we hadn't "forced" elected leaders to take a stand on the issue of narcotics production. It was too easy for them to be on the side of law enforcement when the central government was present and on the side of the narco-traffickers when they were in town.

In terms of weaknesses, we didn't have an endless stream of funding, but we could move faster than the "narcos" if we made some bureaucratic process and supply chain adjustments. We could be transparent, whereas they avoided any disclosure of their activities. We could help establish state presence and offer the citizens, the poor coca farmers, an alternative.

We had a strategy. It was clear. We played to our strengths and took advantage of their weaknesses. We leveraged resources, including the media and government officials, which had not yet been tapped. We used the media to give the image of populous support for peace and security. We engaged elected officials who, many for the first time, took a public position on the issue. We used hard data to dispute or debunk myths propagated by the narco-traffickers. We provided socio-economic assistance through the government of Peru, engaged institutions far and wide, and collected data to bring real facts and figures to the public debate on the issue. In less than two years, together with the government, we changed national public opinion and reduced coca production in Peru. Essentially, our strategy was working, and we had the narco-traffickers looking for coca leaves to make cocaine elsewhere. It was a good strategy, and it worked.

Here's another example. Strategies are used by almost everyone from every walk of life. For instance, I was a high school track and field coach in Terre Haute, Indiana. For each of our track meets, we had a strategy. I remember our biggest track meet, South vs. West Vigo. I coached West Vigo, which had a small, more rural student body. South was the powerhouse with 45 girls on the team; West Vigo had about 16. South sent girls to the state track finals every year; West Vigo never did.

I did the external analysis. I knew every member of South's track team, their events, times, heights, and distances. I tracked them for weeks. I kept a chart. I also knew my girls and their best times and potential. In those days, there were 13 events. I ran my virtual match-ups to get the best results, but concluded, short of a miracle or one of South's key runners being sick that day, we were going to lose. There was simply no way we could win. We didn't have the depth. The key to an upset, even if it didn't mean winning, was focusing on their 4x400 relay team and the last event of the meet. We strategized and planned. On the day of the track meet, we won several events and placed enough to score the points we needed, but there was no way we could win the last event. Everything went precisely as we had planned, so we decided to have a little fun and scare the living daylights out of this powerhouse. I instructed my relay team to hold back and not go to the line until the last call. Going into the last event, we were ahead by three points. This race would decide the outcome. South's coach was shocked and almost panicking. I'll admit I took some pleasure in just watching it. On the third and final call, my 4x400 relay team moved to the starting line. They were my shot-putters! I knew we couldn't win, so I had placed our usual relay team members in other events to pick up points and they did. Our shot-putters were in good shape, because they had trained side by side with the runners from the beginning of the season. They took the line, ran their best, got lapped, but finished strong. I was never so proud of a team. We lost to a powerhouse, but we gave them a real scare. That year, we broke 12 of the 13 girls' track and field records for the high school and we had a lot of fun along the way.

That was an example of strategy. We dealt with the cards we had, knew our competition and the environment, set a vision, developed a plan that took advantage of our strengths, and exploited opportunities.

Once you have the broad outlines of a strategy, you can set realistic objectives and intermediate milestones. Whether you're working with a high school track team, a public-sector program, or a world-class business, the strategy and the elements are fundamentally the same. Winning or achieving the vision begins with a goal—whether it is market share or a reduction in the number of children who go to bed each night hungry. There are many, many small wins that come long before achieving the ultimate vision. These wins come as a result of talent, hard work, skill development, and learning. They come from a little bit of luck and from setting dozens of smaller goals, planning, working, and adjusting to get the incremental or intermediate win.

Establishing Objectives

Once the vision and strategy are in place, your focus should turn toward establishing objectives and subobjectives with timelines and targets. How do you know which objectives, subobjectives, timelines, and targets to set to ensure that your vision and goals are achieved? You draw on an internal analysis of how aligned your major systems are in supporting your vision and goal achievement. Many people use the 7-S framework[19,20], developed by McKinsey & Company with help from Harvard and Stanford Business Schools professors. The aim was to help businesses and organizations identify how best to organize and manage their institutions. The key factor with the 7-S framework is to ensure internal alignment, meaning that all of the internal systems and elements are aligned in support of the vision and goal. The 7 Ss are:

1. Strategy: a set of actions that together will give your organization or company a competitive advantage;

2. Structure: how the institution is organized to carry out the functions to achieve the goal (units, groupings, coordination mechanisms);

3. Systems: processes and procedures for getting the work done, including the reward and promotion, management, budget, policy development, and performance measurement systems, as well as the interconnectedness of these systems;

4. Staffing: the employees, their competencies, how recruitment happens, how careers are managed, how staff members are trained;

5. Skills: expertise, best practices, and distinct competencies;

6. Leadership Style: accepted and used within the organization, titles, how time of executives is distributed, how decisions are made, etc.; and

7. Shared Values: collective, underlying principles of an organization.

If the seven Ss are aligned, the organization will be more effective and/or competitive.

As you can see, the 7-S model is both a great tool for assessing and diagnosing an institution and an extremely practical method of setting targets and timelines for moving closer to complete internal alignment.

Remember, as an executive, your primary function is to bring value by making the organization more effective or the company more competitive. In practice, you begin with the systems and people you have. In a perfect world, you will meet every objective, target, and timeline you establish, but this rarely, if ever, happens. In practice, what happens is that you begin down a path of an iterative process where you celebrate your achievements and take corrective actions to move closer to complete alignment. Keep in mind, complete alignment is an ideal and is never really achieved, but you can come close and you can always improve. As you establish and meet targets, you reestablish the next set of targets working day in and day out, month by month, to get closer to the larger goal and vision. Inevitably, you will miss targets and fall short of objectives. This is where you need to step back, reassess, and ask yourself what is not working, what is possibly out of line. You may need to break an objective or target into smaller steps and incremental goals. You may need to make adjustments, such as move a staff member, so that there is a closer match between the strengths an employee has to offer and the needs of the objective. Sometimes, the employee has the strengths required, but is missing a more difficult to discern attitude, perspective, or personality preference. Most executives simply move the person out of the position. This can backfire. Without coaching and guidance, the employee is likely to feel rejected and face personal crises that could translate into problems for the organization down the road. Remember, just because an employee leaves your company doesn't mean he can't cause harm. Letting someone go on good terms is of the utmost importance. I find that coaching works particularly well in these kinds of situations. Coaching this kind of employee helps him discover what is best for him. It can help him gain a new productive perspective and broader view. Ultimately, if he leaves the company or organization, he does so on good terms.

If targets are missed and units fall short of expectations, something else is missing. For example, maybe the employee doesn't have one of the required elements. When personal goals, objectives, and values align with the organization or company goals, objectives, and values, you are destined to succeed.

Common Problems with Strategies

The problems that often befall visions can similarly be observed in strategies. I've seen large units and institutions that have no strategy or a strategy that isn't clear, because it hasn't been communicated to in a way that can be understood, embraced, and internalized. Having a strategy that isn't clear is as bad as having no strategy at all.

Another common problem with strategies is that they aren't compelling, aren't going to "win," or aren't going to achieve the goals and vision. Obviously, all strategies cannot be brilliant. You can have a strategy that isn't very strong. Perhaps the elements of the strategy don't take advantage of institutional strengths or don't position the company to take advantage of emerging opportunities. Sometimes these strategies aren't compelling because there is a tendency to underestimate institutional weaknesses or to avoid discussion of threats altogether. Sometimes these strategies overestimate internal strengths. Such strategies, even if implemented perfectly, will fail to achieve the vision. The more accurate and objective you can be about these elements, the more likely you are to establish a compelling strategy.

One very common failure I frequently observe in strategies is inaccurate or false assumptions. Strategies are built upon assumptions, and every strategy assumes some risk that is usually expressed in the assumptions made. These assumptions are the conclusions about trends and the future drawn from your external analysis. They must be explicitly stated, but often they aren't. They may have been completely valid and realistic when the vision and strategy were conceived, but have since fallen victim to changing times. Assumptions are the building blocks of strategies—the foundation in many ways. Your job as an executive is to ensure regular, if not constant, updating of these assumptions to make sure that they remain accurate and relevant.

Like vision, sometimes a strategy is "spot on," but the skills required to carry it out are missing or inadequate, the culture is out of sync, or the leadership style is incongruent. The team responsible for particular tactics can be dysfunctional at worst and inefficient at best. Sometimes you don't have the right talent with the right experience or the right orientation for teamwork. These are misalignments, and unless the vision and strategy are aligned with internal systems, including culture, values, leadership style, and skills, the likelihood of falling short is high. In my example of the high school track team, I simply didn't have the skills on the team. Everything else was there, but we fell short of our goal to win because we lacked the skills.

Strategy is dynamic. The shifts in tactics and the setting of subobjectives that feed into larger objectives and weekly, monthly, and yearly goals require that lower-level staff have the flexibility to adjust, as needed, to best achieve their objectives. They can't adjust if they don't understand the vision and the strategy, and they can't adjust if they don't have your trust.

Summary

Establishing a vision and strategy is the responsibility of the executive, although both should be developed with the engagement of many, many others. Setting a clear and motivating vision coupled with an informed and insightful strategy can make all the difference in whether you succeed in leading the company or organization to a more competitive or effective position. The tools for developing strategies and commonly observed issues with strategies that have been discussed in this chapter can help narrow your focus on key aspects. Strategies require constant data collection, review, and adjustment to move ever closer to complete alignment and goal achievement. In Chapter Six, we will talk about the change agenda, the "what" of the strategy, and how you can determine what specifically needs to be changed to achieve the vision.

Chapter Five Secrets

1. Create a vision that: hits the "sweet spot," evokes emotions, is 10 to 20 years in the future, simple and straightforward, and creates a picture.

2. Express risk in assumptions.

3. Capitalize on strengths, minimize weaknesses.

4. The strategy describes the "game plan" for achieving goals and vision.

5. Engage employees in the development of the strategy.

6. Examine alternate scenarios.

7. Strategies are dynamic, especially at the tactical level.

8. Achieving goals and vision is an interactive process.

Chapter Five Exercise

Write down the vision statement of your company or organization. Now apply the characteristics of a good vision to determine how it rates. Submit the corporate or organization's strategy to a peer review. What can you learn from their critiques and suggestions?

Chapter Six

$$\{ \quad \text{BRIDGE THE GAP} \quad \}$$

A change agenda identifies the gap between where you are and where you want to be. It emerges when you identify your vision and goal (where you want to be in the future) and your strategy (how you are going to get there), and compare them to where your company or organization is now. Inevitably, systems will be out of alignment. Certain changes will need to be made in order to achieve the new vision. These needed changes are the change agenda or initiatives.

In highly dynamic work environments, there is a premium on those who can lead change. There aren't that many leaders who can lead change well. In fact, a full 70% of all attempted change ends prematurely, before the change takes hold.[21] Your ability to lead your organization or company to adapt quickly can make all the difference and give your organization the competitive advantage it needs. This chapter reveals the secrets of obtaining that speed and takes a closer look at the advantages of crises and the impediments to speed, particularly in the public sector.

Understanding the Change Process

Your efforts to lead change will be more successful if you understand the change process, how staff reacts to change, and the reasons for typically high rates of failure. Change initiatives have derailed many accomplished leaders, and leading them is perhaps the most difficult part of an executive's job because it requires:

1. Knowledge and understanding of the change process and the key role of trust as a catalyst for change;

2. Awareness of the emotional impact of change on staff and an ability to communicate to the different emotional stages as your people go through them; and

3. Awareness of the five elements of successful change.

You need all three of these to lead a change initiative successfully. Missing one will leave you short of the change you hope to achieve and, therefore, short of your vision and goals.

The Change Process and Trust as a Catalyst for Change

After you have conducted your external and internal analysis and have identified the vision, goal, and strategy, you must then identify what needs to change and articulate the risks involved in not changing, as well as the potential benefits of making the change. Remember, your job is to make your company more competitive or your organization more effective. Therefore, the change agenda or initiative should move your company toward these goals.

The rationale for change is commonly referred to as the "business case for change"; it can be a strong motivator. If people understand the need for change, the importance and benefits of it, they will likely put forth the effort to make the change. For instance, you want the organization to move from a losing or shrinking competitive position to a more competitive position. A business case for change projects into the future and describes what will be different. It positions the company or organization to take advantage of opportunities and lays out the risks of change, both positive and negative. You must be absolutely sure that maintaining the status quo puts the company or organization at a real, tangible disadvantage. You then communicate this message to staff with a sense of urgency, so that they will own the change and engage wholeheartedly in its implementation. This persuasive communication is the golden nugget, the key, the secret. (See Chapter Eight for more about influencing broadly, as well as additional secrets for making impact with communication.)

In terms of leading the change agenda, you must be able to translate the business case for change into personal impact. "If we don't change now, we stand to lose market share," may not be personal enough. More personal might be, "If we don't change now, we may need to lay off staff or dissolve this unit." By being clear about what is at stake for a particular person or group, you create ownership, a willingness to engage, and a sense of urgency among your people to launch a change initiative.

Ownership can be so powerful! Building on the earlier example from my work at USAID, as the director of a standing development program aimed at reducing the production of coca leaves used for making cocaine, my initial analysis drew my attention to the fact that the Peruvians didn't own this problem. They saw the production of coca for export as a U.S. or European problem. However, they were aware neither of the rising levels of cocaine use by Peruvian youth nor of the serious financial and social implications of this rise. They had never taken an accurate measure of the consumption of coca for cultural purposes. Collecting data, they found that local, legal consumption was 10% of the total production, compared to the 90% they had assumed. Thus, they began to understand the coca production problem as a Peruvian problem affecting Peruvians. By working with them, we were able to get the elites, the lawmakers and policymakers, to understand the cost of coca production in terms of its impact on their national image, tourism, pubic expenditures, the future of their youth, their overburdened judicial system, and their environment. Then, and only then, did the Peruvians begin to own the cocoa problem. Once they did, they were motivated to act in their own interest and made significant changes quickly.

What is the next step after you've made a convincing and realistic business case for change, created a sense of urgency, and motivate people to engage around the change initiative? Now you must ensure that all internal systems support the vision, goals, and strategy. You might think that the change agenda includes a long list of major steps, which will be led by your senior team and should be implemented quickly within a definitive, short timeline. Wrong!

Trust Is the Secret Ingredient

All leaders, especially new leaders, with a change agenda and marching orders should go slowly. "What? Slowly? How can that be?" Is this completely counterintuitive? Not really. The catalyst for change is a level of trust between the leader, those implementing the change, and those who will be affected by the change. You must, absolutely must, build trust with your staff and your stakeholders, and this takes time. Without trust, you will fail. Full stop. No ifs, ands, or buts. Your first and most important job with regard to leading change is to build trust. It is the key to everything you are responsible for as an executive to bringing about change and communicating the vision, goals, and strategy.

Trust is built in small moments, in small steps. It is built with words and actions. It isn't something you do once and then check the box that it is completed. You build trust day in and day out, in every conversation, speech, and meeting. It is communicated not only with words, but with actions and body language. Your efforts at building trust have to be genuine. Your staff can and will detect even the slightest disingenuousness on your part. You cannot pretend and build trust.

You must be comfortable with the people you surround yourself with because, as an executive, they are your "trust agents." They convey what is important to you and how you think and feel. If they misrepresent your intentions, that is a "trust buster."

Trust is built by slowing down. Literally, walking through the halls more slowly, noticing things and people. It is built by reaching out to staff and stakeholders. It is built by asking, "How are you?" and meaning it. It is built by devoting your full attention to the person in your office without multitasking. It is built by being present and emoting a warm and safe presence, by insisting that employees leave the office on time and only stay late if occasionally absolutely necessary. Having compassionate conversations, whether asking about family or giving critical feedback, builds trust. Building trust requires you to be vulnerable, with a level of maturity and experience that means often putting others before yourself. Trust conveys, "I care about you," and "I am here for you."

While you may diligently build trust day in and day out, you can lose it as well. However, if you have built and continue to build trust, your efforts may be rewarded with "the benefit of the doubt." I once had a student who talked about making "trust deposits" in a "trust account" with the notion that at some point you will intentionally or unintentionally make a withdrawal. It's life, we are people, and we are fallible. Regardless of our best intentions, we will hurt feelings and lose trust now and then. We can prepare for these lapses by continually making deposits into our trust accounts.

If your values and priorities and those of your company or organization are not aligned, you will have a difficult time building trust. It is virtually impossible to build the levels of trust you will need if you are not genuinely committed to the values and priorities of the organization. It is advantageous if you are oriented toward these values before taking the executive position; however, to the extent that your values or motives don't align with those of the company or organization, you should consider either not taking the job or changing yourself before taking the position.

If you think all this talk about trust sounds a lot like love, you may be right. You see, human emotions are contagious. It only takes one person to ignite a chain reaction of human emotion, be it negative or positive. When it is positive, it looks a lot like (and, over time, can actually become) love. This is great, because love is perhaps the most powerful emotion and it can move mountains. Love emits a spirit within an organization that creates amazing positive energy. And positive begets positive! Before you know it, people are working together as one team. Only by working together are they capable of achieving a whole greater than the sum of the parts: think championship athletic teams, Broadway theater ensembles, or the cast and crew of an Oscar-winning film.

Working together with the spirit of love and trust, you and your team can achieve transformational change, which is the goal of every CEO, president, and executive leader. So if you have a lot to do, a big change agenda, and tremendous time pressures, slow down and invest time in your people. Engage them in the process and change will happen fast. Trust and engage your people, and without a doubt, they will exceed your expectations.

Engage your staff early in the development of your vision, the external and internal assessment, and the strategy. This engenders trust, builds ownership, and is a significant factor in successful change management. Although you have taken more time to engage staff up front, the payoff is their support (not their surprise) as you implement change. This type of collaborative change has an energy and potential that mandatory change does not. You'll also find that technology enables you to get input from any corner of the company that you want. Widen the engagement as far as feasible, and use technology to help keep your staff engaged, monitor their acceptance of change, and give them a voice in it. If you do this, the chances are very high that they will trust and support you and the initiative.

How Do You Know If You Have Trust in the Workplace?

Since trust is catalytic to leading a change agenda, you want to make sure you have it. Table 6.1 offers a list of indicators of trust and lack of trust. Look for these signs in your people to judge the level of trust within your company or organization.

Table 6.1: Indicators of High and Low Levels of Trust	
Indicators of High Trust	**Indicators of Low Trust**
Productivity is high.	"Water cooler talk" (people get quiet as you approach).
Innovation is high.	There is little or no quality feedback given.
Attrition is low.	There is little or no challenge to decisions that are made.
Good, honest, growth-promoting feedback is shared routinely.	There is no discussion of differences of opinion, assumptions, or rationale leading to decisions.
Diversity produces disagreements and civil arguments focused on product or process or decision improvement.	The discussion of issues begins after the meeting ends.
Staff members report errors and learn from them.	There is no buy-in, enthusiasm, or risk-taking for innovation.
Staff members socialize (together and with their families) off hours.	There is little or no socializing among staff.
The line between work and private life is blurred because values are aligned.	Either no one or everyone is working late.
	Staff members are missing their children's activities.
	Staff members think the boss isn't working hard enough or question how she spends her time.
	Staff members misinterpret executives' or leaders' intentions or motives.
	There is an empty front row in staff meetings or all-hands meetings.

There are many experts, theories, and tools that describe the change process. They all boil down to four key steps:

1. Build trust early, even before you take the job, if possible;

2. Articulate the business case for change;

3. Sell the business case to those who will be affected by it; and

4. Stand firm and follow through with the change until it is materialized.

The Emotional Impact of Change

People react to change similarly to how they react to death. Generally, you will see people go through six phases: confusion, anger, denial, bargaining, acceptance, and adaptation. What the steps are is less important than knowing that there are different stages that occur in a certain sequence and that individuals move through them at different rates. Also, initial reactions are different than feelings in later stages of implementing change. At first, some people fear change because they can't envision the future; the uncertainty is unsettling for them. Others may have a stake in maintaining the status quo, and so resist any change. Different people react differently to hearing of impending changes.

For this reason, keep in mind the potential damage that a mishandled change agenda can wreak before you launch. The emotional impact of failure cannot be wiped away. By ignoring the lingering emotional impact of a failed change agenda, we may harm the very people we need and are charged with developing. Imagine that despite the energy you have devoted to implementing change, the initiatives repeatedly fail or fall short. How enthusiastic would you be for the next initiative?

Repeated Change Takes a Toll

Research has firmly demonstrated the cumulative effects of experiencing repeated changes. It appears, not surprisingly, that "experiencing repeated, intense changes,"[22] has a negative effect. One of the most common effects is an increase in stress and frustration."[23] This is understandable. As a new executive, you need to be acutely aware that before you took your position, there were many leaders. Some provided little engagement and a lot of direction and the initiatives failed. These repeated unsuccessful attempts have taken a toll on the organization, especially the senior staff members, who understand the issues and know how to gain alignment, but have not received support from leadership. You must understand what change attempts your company or organization has been through in the past several years so that you have a sense of the obstacles you may face and can prepare your communication to address those concerns.

I suspect that a reason for the high failure rate of change initiatives rests in the notion that the executive is required to deal with the different emotional states in so many groups of employees at any given time. This is extremely difficult to manage both cognitively and emotionally and causes some leaders to simply avoid these emotional details of the change process.

To work through the emotional impact of change, a leader must first be aware of the emotional stages of change mentioned previously: confusion, anger, denial, bargaining, acceptance, and adaptation. The leader must recognize these emotional stages when she sees them manifested, and she must know how to tailor communications to address her team's concerns. Finally, she needs to understand that this is normal. More often than not, executives have some notion of the disruptive nature of change, but are inadequately prepared to handle the sequenced and layered stages that happen simultaneously in all levels of the organization or company.

Figure 6.1: Illustrative Change Patterns

	Year 1				Year 2				Year 3	
	Q1 Change Announced	Q2 Change Sold	Q3 Change Decisions	Q4 Change	Q1 Change Completed	Q2	Q3	Q4	Q1	Q2
Senior Leader	Confusion	Anger	Denial	Bargain	Accept	Adapt	Achieve Change	Achieve Change		
Senior Managers		Confusion	Anger	Denial	Bargain	Accept	Adapt	Adapt	Achieve Change	
Divisional Managers			Confusion	Anger	Denial	Bargain	Accept	Accept		
Supervisors				Confusion	Anger	Denial	Bargain	Accept	Achieve Change	
Employees					Anger	Denial	Bargain	Accept	Adapt	Achieve Change

"The Change Management Conference: Disciplined, Analytical and Practical Approaches to Managing High Stakes Change June 21-22, 2012, New York, NY."

Figure 6.1 illustrates this multilayered challenge. For example, your company may have five layers of management under the executive:

1. Senior team

2. Senior managers

3. Divisional managers

4. Supervisors

5. Staff members

Each level receives the news of change at a different time. Those closest to the top hear it first, usually before the town hall or all-hands meeting. Chances are that the executive will fall short of making the business case for change or of selling it to the supervisors or employees. So, the senior team and senior managers hear of the change before this formal communiqué, and they have time to work their way through the confusion stage. They may have moved through the anger stage into the denial stage while the division managers are just entering the anger stage. The supervisors, having just heard the news for the first time, are confused and have questions. The employees at the meeting where the change was announced probably didn't even register the change.

So what's happening here? The executive believes he has announced, made the business case, and sold the change to his key stakeholders, including all his staff. In actuality, a couple weeks shy of reporting to the board that the change has been adopted, you'll hear a different story from every level in the organization when you ask them about the change initiative.

If you are skilled at handling these stages, you know that your job is to roll up your sleeves and communicate, communicate, communicate! Internal communications are paramount. Listen. Don't assume that no noise is good news. When people are angry, they tend to be loud. When they are in denial, they tend to get quiet. Listen for cues about where your people are emotionally in response to change. Know that these reactions (whatever they might be) are normal, and communicate with your people. Address their concerns, clarify assumptions, share the rationale behind the initiative with them, engage them in decisions, and paint a picture of a better future. Above all, stay engaged.

Your job doesn't stop at creating a change agenda, making the business case, and selling it. The last step of implementing the initiative is to ensure that not only is the vision clear, but also that you have the right staff, incentives, resources, and plans in place. These constitute the five essential elements of successful change. If you are missing one of these, your change initiative will likely stall or fail.

Get the Right Staff in the Right Place

Some experts will advise starting with understanding how comfortable your staff is with change. They may advise you to identify the change agents and use them strategically to bring the others along. We know that some people are simply averse to change. They are not bad people. They simply take more convincing before they get on board. Know that reluctance is okay and give them time to work through the issues. Supply them with the information and rationale they need. Give them time. They will eventually get on board or decide to leave. Waiting is okay with one exception. If the late adapter is in a critically important leadership position, if you need this person to help lead the change agenda, then waiting will not work. You have to deal with this head on. Circumstances will dictate what to do. Sometimes the person will come aboard, and sometimes it's just not a good fit and they will be happier elsewhere. Again, this is okay. It's a part of change.

Five Essential Elements of Successful Change

Before change begins, your job is to provide specific information about each of the five essential change elements to those charged with implementation. By detailing these, you reduce the risk of failure or abandonment. If any of these are not in place before you embark, then there is a high probability that the change will fail and/or be unsustainable. The five essential elements are:

1. The vision and corresponding goals;

2. The right people with the right skills in place;

3. The incentive(s) to motivate the change;

4. Sufficient resources to fully implement the change; and

5. A plan that details the steps of the change process.

Figure 6.2 illustrates these five essential elements: vision, skills, incentives, resources, and a plan. The last column in the figure, "If missing, result is..." reveals the common side effects of a missing element. For instance, if you have the right skills and incentives, adequate resources, and an action plan, but the vision is not clear, the result is confusion. Perhaps you have all of the elements except the right skills. If so, your organization or unit will exhibit anxiety. If everything is in place but the right incentives, the effect will be slow implementation. Frustration results when everything is in place except adequate resources and you'll detect a number of starts and stops when a clear action plan is missing.

Figure 6.2: Elements of a Successful Change
All Five Are Needed

Vision	Skills	Incentives	Resources	Action Plan	If missing, the result is:
	X	X	X	X	Confusion
X		X	X	X	Anxiety
X	X		X	X	Slowness
X	X	X		X	Frustration
X	X	X	X		False Starts

The Change Management Conference: Disciplined, Analytical and Practical Approaches to Managing High Stakes Change June 21-22, 2012, New York, NY."

The way to ensure a greater probability of success, then, is to detail these five elements to the company or organization and specifically to the team tasked with leading the change. Lay it out for them. Don't assume people know what needs to be done. Do this by giving them the answers to the following questions:

- Which skills and which people are assigned to implement the change?

- Who has what role?

- How will people be rewarded?

- What incentives will be used?

- What resources will be applied where?

- Are there sufficient resources available in a timely manner to achieve the change?

- What master action plan will staff use as their guide?

Your staff needs you to answer these questions in detail. Your level of clarity will help ensure that the change agenda or initiative proceeds without a hitch.

Crisis Can Force Change

Crises can force change like nothing else. We've all heard the saying that "sometimes you have to have a breakdown before you can have a breakthrough." If you are fired from your job or get passed over for a promotion, you face a personal crisis. If you suffer a serious health episode like a heart attack or cancer diagnosis, urgency has been created. It causes you to do a lot of honest introspection and to focus on the most important aspects of your life. It forces you to change, hopefully for the better. Institutions are the same. When a company is faced with a crisis, it usually brings in new leadership and triggers a top-to-bottom review that results in learning, a new or renewed direction and sense of purpose, and an accompanying list of factors that need to change to put the institution back on the right track.

When change is forced upon an organization, e.g., in a crisis, a rapid negative change, or a failed initiative, it creates urgency. For example, the financial crisis of 2008 resulted in increased government regulation of the housing and banking sectors. The tragic events of September 11th fundamentally changed the way we fight wars and yielded a new government entity, the Department of Homeland Security. Natural disasters have forced change upon the Federal Emergency Management Administration (FEMA). When the General Accounting Office (GAO) or the Inspector General (IG) issue a scathing report, it creates a business case for change and urgency. Crises have a way of delivering a sense of urgency to leaders in ways that business as usual cannot. In other words, people aren't likely to change unless the force is sufficient enough to cause movement.

You can see this in companies as well. During his tenure as J.C. Penney's CEO, Ron Johnson, who was brought in to turn the company's downward trend around, posted a dismal track record of 25% lower sales and a net loss of nearly one billion dollars. Instead of increasing market share, the company was losing it quickly. It didn't take Penney's long to figure out that Johnson's strategy wasn't working and the former CEO was brought back to bring the company into balance. Clearly, Penney's acted quickly in a crisis. Whether or not replacing a new CEO with a former CEO was the best decision will be determined in the coming years. The point is that the board reacted quickly because of the sense of urgency created by the crisis.

Corporate mergers create tremendous urgency to adopt or adapt in creating a new entity. Mergers can create opportunities as well as result in significant layoffs. These are powerful motivators for change and create a sense of urgency. Another common crisis is product tampering. This was the case for Johnson & Johnson during the 1982 Tylenol® scare, when seven people in Chicago died after ingesting cyanide-laced Tylenol® capsules. The company's market share dropped from 37% before the tampering to only 7% after. It forced the Federal Drug Administration (FDA) and Johnson & Johnson to protect consumers by mandating tamper-resistant packaging that most of us now take for granted.

Change Agendas in Government

Crises bring a level of urgency to a company that business as usual cannot. It is important for leaders to take advantage of crises, viewing them as potential accelerators of change. This is particularly true in government, when political leadership remains in a position for only 18-24 months, on average, and crises of any nature can be an opportunity to accelerate the change agenda.

In general, change in the public sector is slow. There are a number of reasons for this. It can be hard to sell if career public employees perceive that a part of the criteria for change is politically driven. In government, it can be arduous and time consuming to get the right people with the right skills in place. Just getting a job created, classified, and announced can take many months. Then staff must sift through applicants, conduct interviews, select a candidate, gain security clearances, and satisfy the many other requirements of civil service jobs. Once hired, the new employee must go through initial training or orientation, and so on. That's why in the federal government it can take 18 months or more to have the right person with the right skills in the right job.

As with staffing, moving resources and developing plans take far more time than in the private sector. Because Congress appropriates public funds, movement requires consultation at a minimum, and sometimes legislation. If the change you want to bring about requires funding, then in many cases you need to gain support from your appropriators in Congress. It can easily take two years before you have new funds and the political support from elected leaders to make the change you believe is necessary to be more effective.

Now that you have the funds, you will need to spend the money. In government, this involves issuing contracts and following a federally regulated procurement process. Depending on the initiative, the change, and the size of the procurement, this can take a full year and often more.

The bottom line is that it takes time to initiate and carry out significant change in the federal government. Political leaders, especially those who don't have this basic understanding, can run into a brick wall fast and get frustrated. I believe that this, in part, accounts for the relatively brief tenure in public leadership positions. Also, political leaders who don't know how to manage the emotional stages of change cascading through an organization can easily fall into the trap of believing that career staff is hostile to them or their ideas. While this isn't likely, career staff may be hostile to the notion that their leader is not well prepared to lead the change or initiative they desire. Sometimes, an executive's political aspirations become part of the hidden argument for change. Career staff members are able to sense this ambition and, in general, will dislike the leader who puts ambition into the business case for change. Staff sees this as disingenuous and it is a big buster of the very trust a leader needs to carry out the change agenda.

Summary

Once you have conducted your external and internal assessments and developed your vision, goal, and strategy, you are in a position to establish a change agenda. Thoroughly study previous change agendas and their fate. Why did they succeed or fail? What lasting imprint did they leave on your institution, your staff, and people throughout the organization? Communicate to and engage with your staff to understand the business case for change and create a sense of urgency. Remember the five essential elements of change and emotional stages of change and communicate the elements and tailor messages to the emotional stages. Don't go too fast at first and remember, to the extent feasible, engage staff in these processes. Finally, acknowledge that change takes longer than most leaders assume. Part of the reason it takes so long is that culture is a powerful, invisible force that absolutely must be understood and accounted for. In Chapter Seven, we will take a closer look at corporate culture to understand why it is so important to the change agenda and why it is so tough to change.

Chapter Six Secrets

1. Understand the change management process and associated emotional reactions and ensure that all requirements for successful change are met before beginning the change process.

2. Start slow. Take time, all the time it takes, to build trust in your staff and stakeholders. Only then will you be able to implement change quickly enough to achieve your agenda, goals, and vision.

3. Know the indicators of trust and a lack of trust to understand and judge how quickly the institution can change.

4. Learn how to detect and communicate with people who may be at different emotional stages of change.

5. Articulate to your staff the five essential elements (vision, skills, incentives, resources, plan) needed to bring about change. Don't assume they know these.

6. View a crisis or breakdown as an opportunity for change. Oftentimes you have to break down and face a crisis, a setback, or a disappointment before you can break through and set a new course, reinvigorate your commitment, and learn.

Chapter Six Exercise

Review the indicators of trust and mistrust. For one week, observe the staff around you both in meetings and informally and note whether their behavior falls into the trust or mistrust category. Ask four other people of varying levels of responsibility to make the same observations and behavioral assessments for one week. Collect the data and discuss its implications.

Chapter Seven

{ # THE MOTHER OF ALL SYSTEMS }

Given how important corporate culture is to achieving change and implementing strategy, we're going to explore it further. To an outsider, culture may not seem that important, but understanding it is crucial to your success as an executive leader. Your first question might be, what is culture? Like executive leadership, it is hard to define. Edgar Schein, former professor at MIT's Sloan School of Management and leader in the field of organizational development and culture, offers this definition, "The deeper level of basic assumptions and beliefs that are shared by members of an organization, that operate subconsciously, and that define a basic 'taken for granted' fashion and organization's view of itself and its environment."[24] Clear? I bet not.

What about this definition put forward by two important academic leaders in organizational development and culture (based at Stanford University School of Business), Charles O'Reilly and Jennifer

Chatman: "A system of shared values (that define what is important) and norms that define appropriate attitudes and behaviors for organizational members (how to feel and behave)."[25] Is that better?

In my work, I like to use the simple definition, "That's just the way we do things around here." This is the pat response newcomers so frequently hear when asked why things are done a certain way. Basically what it says is, "This is our culture. We can't explain it. You just need to assimilate and fast!"

Culture is an organization's collective and normed belief system. It is the values system. Linda Ford, another thought leader in organizational development, refers to corporate culture as "the invisible force that compels compliance,"[26] especially for newcomers. The culture manifests itself in "the way things are done" or the behaviors, traditions, and folklore of the organization. These are not written down anywhere, yet they are more important than any rulebook or book of procedures. If you don't understand this, you are destined to misstep at a very minimum, and at worst you'll be bucked off the cultural bronco and out of the organization's rodeo.

How can something that is so hard to define, that can't be seen or measured, be so important? It is counterintuitive, which may be why culture is probably the toughest element to change in organizations and the most difficult to understand. Every organization has a different culture; there's no basic handbook that can apply everywhere. So, as a leader, how do you know if a culture change is needed? And if you do know that a culture change is needed, who is going to change it?

As an example, let's compare the corporate cultures at the Department of State and USAID, two separate, but linked, federal government entities that work extremely closely together. Previous leaders have tried, unsuccessfully, to merge USAID into the Department of State, but it is, in fact, happening slowly and incrementally. Many cite cultural differences as an obstacle to merging and the staff certainly feel those differences in culture when they work together. See Table 7.1 for a comparison of the two cultures.

Table 7.1: Cultures of the Department of State and USAID		
Cultural Element	**Department of State**	**USAID**
Structure	Hierarchy respected	Flat structure
Communications	Subtle	Direct
Objective time horizon	Short-term	Long-term
Planning	Ad hoc	Detailed, process
Primary function	Manage perceptions/image	Manage programs
Frame of reference	Political frame of reference	Technical frame
Hires	Generalist	Technical specialist
Values	Good records/history	Scientific process/lessons
Operations	Centralized	Decentralized
Primary client	Foreign policy goals	Developing country

Just from this brief comparison, it's easy to see the many problems that can occur when two organizations interact. Conflict is inevitable without exceptionally strong communication and a willingness on both sides to adjust in order to accommodate their individual cultures. Working collaboratively can take significantly more time, because such things as perspectives, values, structure, and style are not shared between the two organizations. As a result, many erroneous assumptions can be made that lead to false conclusions about what drives behaviors and interactions. Misunderstandings abound!

An example of this can be seen in the production and use of the Department of State's Mission Performance Plan (MPP), an annual report on the performance of foreign policy, including foreign assistance and upcoming plans, that was introduced around 2003. It is meant to capture incremental changes or progress in all U.S. government investments including foreign policy, foreign assistance, and personnel. It is designed to report against a set of indicators annually. Both the Department of State and USAID staff agreed with the value of creating an ability to report impacts of the sum total of all government investments in an embassy or post overseas. Although it is intended to be a product with shared ownership across government, the MPP has typically been viewed by USAID staff as a Department of State product imposed from the center with no input from the field. However, for the Department of State, this was the normal way of doing business, i.e., to receive direction from headquarters and respectfully execute as directed by the hierarchy. USAID staff saw the MPP as ad hoc, not carefully planned, extraneous to its existing planning systems and procedures, and with no consequence for its budget. Some would go as far as to argue that having crafted indicators without a means to measure them annually was an example of why this didn't make any technical sense. The Department of State staff quickly interpreted the MPP as a political tool, which didn't necessarily need to make technical sense. USAID staff was reluctant to participate in the production of this product, because so much about the MPP and the way it was introduced was inconsistent with the USAID culture. Glaring cultural differences in structure, planning, dominant frames of reference, communications, values, and operations were revealed in this MPP example. As a result of both institutions' inability to deal with their cultural differences, USAID staff never wholeheartedly embraced the change, Department of State employees put as little time as possible into the production of the MPP, rendering it of little use to anyone.

Nowhere, perhaps, is culture more obvious than when you set foot in a foreign country. The language may be different, the accent certainly is, and you can observe cultural differences everywhere by what is said, how people act, and how they interact. For instance, what time do people get up in the morning? What time do they arrive at work? I remember being in Colombia and Peru, where people didn't stir until eight or nine in the morning.

In Cambodia, people get up with the sun around six a.m. or so. They are out sweeping their front walks and streets in the early morning. Could cleanliness be linked to pride in their culture? What does that tell you about the culture? Cambodians eat a hot bowl of noodles for breakfast, often at a local restaurant. What does that tell you about the culture? Dress in the workplace is typically casual. However, in Peru, even the drivers wear suits. Suits and formality are signs of respect. In one country, people report to work at 8 a.m. on the dot or they are considered late. In another, country people show up to work anywhere between 8 and 10 a.m. and they aren't late. What does this difference tell you about how time is viewed in these different cultures?

In Senegal, during meetings, everyone was given a chance to speak and only at the end would the oldest, most senior person speak. Without fail, whether the meeting was in the office or in a village with members of the community, the oldest, most senior person spoke last. What does this tell you about age in this culture? It should tell you that seniority and age command respect. The Senegalese value the knowledge that comes with experience. Also, the fact that everyone was given a chance to speak demonstrates that they operate on the basis of consensus.

In India, the meetings were completely different. Not everyone spoke. Those who did would openly argue and talk over each other. The age or seniority of the person speaking didn't matter as much as did their class or caste. Women in villages rarely spoke at gatherings with outsiders. The discussion tended to follow an unwritten code of who was more important and who mattered most. While the caste system is becoming more obsolete, it still functions. By your last name alone, Indians can infer your caste, class, and the geographic origins of your family. How does that cultural factor weigh in the workplace? Lower-level castes typically won't speak in a meeting of higher-ranking people, unless specifically asked. Historically, Indians assigned value to occupations and backgrounds in a way that few other cultures have. Again, this is changing, but slowly, as leaders start to recognize it as a distinct disadvantage for their country.

The power of culture can be seen in significant, though small, interactions. I remember my first overseas job in Bamako, Mali. During my first days, I needed service from a clerk. I went to her desk and said, "Could you please process my travel paperwork?" She didn't stop what she was doing. She didn't look up. I waited politely thinking that she just needed to finish up a small task that she was engaged in before she could devote time to my request. After about five minutes of standing by her desk, I said, "I see you're busy. I'll come back." She said nothing. I was so new to the office; I couldn't imagine I had done anything to annoy her. After a couple of hours, I went back to her desk for a repeat performance and result. By this time I was frustrated. I went back in the afternoon to the same clerk's desk. Someone had arrived right before me, and as I listened, I noticed that he seemed to be getting the service he expected. He was engaged in a full two-minute conversation about the clerk, her family, the weather, and so on. When it was my turn, I mimicked him, inquiring of the clerk, "How are you? How is your family?" This led to a more personal conversation. Only after a couple minutes of conversation did she say, "How can I help you?" I learned an important lesson that day: the importance of understanding culture to getting anything done. In Mali, the culture values people, their families, and their health. They don't take it for granted that everyone is healthy and happy (which makes sense in a country with high maternal mortality and child deaths from preventable diseases). Also, because the country is so dependent on rain for food production and agriculture, key components of the economy are rain and weather. From that moment forward during my stay in Mali, I began every request with a minute or two of conversation about health, family, and the weather. This small investment made a world of difference in getting things done and it taught me a lot about culture.

Seek to Understand the Culture

As an executive leader, particularly if you are new to the company or organization, do you assimilate or do they? It should be you. For instance, if they wear suits and ties or dresses, so do you. If they start and stop meetings on time, so do you. If they all take lunch at the same time, so do you. It may sound counterintuitive, but you will lose valuable insights into corporate culture if you demand conformity to your way of doing things before you understand the established culture. Shocking them by bucking it and insisting they conform to you is not likely to work. It is okay to be different, but don't insist. Choose your battles very carefully while you are learning your way around this new culture.

As an executive, you need to observe the corporate culture of your company or organization. You need to understand what drives it. What are its underlying assumptions? How important is reshaping it to achieving your vision, goals, and strategy? If the answer is, "It is critical to achieving the vision," then take actions using your systems to alter behavior and address assumptions and beliefs. If the answer is "not critical," then don't try and change it. Culture is deeply engrained and based in assumptions, values, and beliefs. Changing those things is an incredibly difficult endeavor. Trying to change the way people think about time, money, individualism, or historical legacies is not something you should approach without a healthy dose of empathy, humility, and caution.

How do you understand culture? Keen observational skills and genuine curiosity about how and why things are done in a particular way is a good start. Pay attention to behaviors that make up the unwritten code of culture. Observe the items in the Cultural Assessment Questionnaire (Exhibit 7.1) closely to understand these behaviors and what they tell you about corporate culture.

Exhibit 7.1: Cultural Assessment Questionnaire

- What is the rhythm of the work?
- What are the normal work hours?
- How do people communicate? Through email? At the water cooler or coffee pot?
- Are slides used in presentations or are presentations oral brief or discussion style?
- Do staff members go to the boss' office or does the boss go to them?
- What are the most popular stories and what do they tell you about culture?
- What are the traditions or rituals? How are new employees welcomed, or not?
- How do policies get made?
- What do the formal written statements, charters, or philosophies say?
- How were those formal statements developed?
- What are the unwritten rules?
- What ceremonial traditions are there for promotions or retirements?
- How do staff members view conflict and is there open arguing?
- Are there group photos posted? Family photos?
- What is on the walls?
- Where do people eat lunch?
- Is there an allowance for exercise time?
- How easy is it for an outsider to get into your office space?

Needless to say, the way you go about collecting this information is subtle and takes time. You may not hear the answers at first. Observe. Ask questions and listen closely to the responses. When people respond with, "That's the way it's always been done," "That's how we do things around here," or "I don't know. It just is," then you know you've hit upon a core value or belief. Your job is to ensure that the culture aligns to support the vision, goals, and strategy. Only if it does not should you attempt to gradually reshape it in that direction. It is an exercise in humility and one that must be approached gingerly and incrementally.

Change Culture Only If You Must

Executives can shape culture, if needed, but it takes a long time. Before you try to change the culture, take the time to understand it, the rationale behind it, and the entrenched interest in conserving it. You need to know what you are up against before you try to change the culture. Assuming that you do see a need to change an aspect of the culture, how you go about it is key to sustaining the change. As the executive, you can shape the culture in the same manner you would introduce any change. Analyze the objectives. Identify cultural norms that are not aligned with the vision and goals. Align the objectives and changes that need to be made and then encourage employees to change via the use of incentives such as reward systems. In doing so, you can shape the culture into one that is more healthy, productive, and aligned with the vision.

If you are unable to lead the shaping of the culture, it could be your downfall, as it has been for thousands of leaders before you. Many executives focus on changing overt behaviors and not the underlying beliefs, values, and assumptions that keep a culture in place. Behavioral change is only temporary and old behaviors will appear and slide back into alignment with the culture. This is a major challenge for government executives. The average tenure of politically appointed executives is between one-and-a-half and two years, not enough time to change culture. The employees know this and they simply wait for the executive to leave. Attempts to change culture in this environment are met with conforming behavior, but this does not fundamentally change the culture. Changing the culture takes years—years that politically appointed executives typically do not spend in office. The relatively short length of tenure of executives in the federal government is an impediment to achieving not only cultural alignment, but by extension, to instituting policies and programs. More often than not, politically appointed executives become frustrated with their inability to implement transformative initiatives and policies. They believe the bureaucracy moves too slowly, and sometimes it does. Yet, it is also true that an adept executive who understands the importance of culture to the vision, goals, and strategy will know how to shape the culture and make significant and more rapid gains.

It seems that every federal government executive who takes a new position aspires to lead a transformational change. The challenge is that some of these new executives have no idea what this means, what it entails, how long it will take, nor how to bring it about. As a result, they typically leave after a couple of years frustrated, burnt-out, and puzzled about why they couldn't move the mountain. These executives underestimated what it takes to change culture and overestimated their role in changing it. You see, government executives actually have a very limited influence on culture. Unless they are willing to commit many more years than is average for a politically appointed executive, their impact might be nil. You can see that executives need to have a good understanding of culture and its power in determining whether the culture must change to achieve the vision. With acute listening and observational skills to interpret misalignments, and trust with and from the workforce, the executive can begin to shape the culture needed to support the vision. Experienced executives in government focus on more a modest vision with goals of two or three of the most important initiatives while taking actions to gradually influence the culture.

Practically speaking, allocation of rewards is a powerful incentive to change deeply rooted culture. Rewards aren't just monetary rewards, although money is a powerful incentive. Rewards can include access to the leader, status, and proximity of workspace to leader, visibility, and awards. The allocation of resources can be another powerful incentive for modifying culture. Executives can also, as with any change, identify the change agents and highlight publicly their new behaviors that are consistent with the culture needed to attain the vision. Executives can use the power of their communication to create and highlight new stories, traditions, or rituals. There are many other creative ways to shape culture to align it with the vision and goals and it is the executive's job to lead that effort.

Learn from the mistakes of others when it comes to shaping culture. Whatever you do, don't delegate it and certainly don't delegate it to one person. Changing culture is the mother of all change initiatives and all the principles that apply to the management of your change agenda apply here. Be transparent. Address issues. Measure progress. Stay engaged. It really is that important!

Build a Team Culture

Part of shaping culture is to create a high-achieving internal environment or to build an esprit de corps, a team spirit. This spirit goes beyond the individual and accounts for a team whose whole is greater than the sum of its parts. It is the executive leader's job to focus on building this spirit as part of shaping culture. If you look in the stands of the winning basketball team at the end of a championship, listen to the ovation from the audience after a breathtaking performance, or witness the energetic displays of shareholders after the close of the stock market, the launch of a new product, or the acquisition of a new company, you'll see this spirit. It is hard to measure because it is intangible, yet it is easy to observe.

But where does the team begin and end? It begins with you: Cheerleader-in-chief! Staff members look to their leader to be the cheerleader, team captain, and coach. Where does the team end? Does it end with the employees, the board, the customers, the stakeholders, or the partners? Essentially, what encompasses "team" depends on how big you dream, on what you want to accomplish. In most large companies, and certainly in most of the federal government, today, the team extends far beyond the walls of their buildings. That's because these leaders understand that collaborating has a greater long-term benefit than competing. It is counterintuitive, especially if you are talking about collaborating with your competitors, but before you disregard it, think about it. Reframe the scope of your job. What is it and who is it that you are leading? What do you want or need to accomplish to be successful? You'll find that more can be accomplished by collaborating than competing. The esprit de corps that is so elusive is also extremely contagious, especially among collaborators working toward the same goal and vision.

Without putting priority on and committing to creating a culture conducive to a "team spirit" atmosphere, your organization or company is destined not to fulfill its potential. If teammates don't really get to know each other, their strengths and weaknesses, concerns and dreams, then the team will underutilize individuals' knowledge, experience, and expertise. As the executive, you are responsible for this unfulfilled potential.

Some leaders rely on employee data to measure progress on proxy indicators for the "team spirit" atmosphere. One caution here: the data from employee surveys is only as good as the level of trust in the atmosphere. Typically, an organization that suffers from elements of dysfunction also suffers from an inhibition of expression of honest feedback—the very same feedback that is needed to make serious strides. In these environments, the data will almost always be tilted toward the positive and mask the severity of underlying issues. See Table 7.2 for true indicators of cohesive teams.

Table 7.2: Indicators of Cohesive Teams
They eat lunch together and socialize in off hours
Gratitude flows are multidirectional
Feedback flows are multidirectional
Laughter flows are multidirectional
They support each other in work and outside work with life events, such as ill children, death of parent, personal achievements
There aren't side-bar discussions, but one conversation in meetings
Ideas flow multidirectionally and build off of each other
There aren't disparaging comments, looks, or body language

Pace of Work as Part of Culture

This is an aspect of leadership where otherwise smart and committed people stumble. There is no manual on this aspect of leadership, just like there is no manual informing a coach how hard to push his athletes. It is learned by doing, making mistakes, and adjusting. It has a lot to do with leadership style and fundamental philosophies about human nature. It is part of the internal environment. At USAID, I pushed my staff to strive for excellence. I believed in them. In hindsight, perhaps I pushed too hard in some cases. I wasn't personally ambitious, but rather ambitious for the mission and for the agency. I believed that the goal of reducing poverty worldwide was laudable, worthy, and achievable. I believed my staff could achieve more than they ever thought possible. In most cases, I was right, and they surprised even themselves. I believe this is true in general. I believe humans will, in most cases, meet and exceed expectations. So it's best to learn, adjust, and move forward wiser because of the experience.

Summary

Culture is the mother of all systems, and it is perhaps the most difficult to assess and certainly the most difficult to alter. An executive must understand the culture before she can begin to shape it. Her job is to reshape it only if necessary and only to the extent that such change will benefit the strategy and aid in obtaining the institutional goals and vision. A culture of genuine teamwork has the potential to aid transformational change.

The importance of executive communication cannot be underestimated when driving strategy and implementing a change agenda within an institution. Internal communication is a reflection of culture, and as such, it is important for the executive to communicate in ways that are culturally appropriate, as I will explain in Chapter Eight.

Chapter Seven Secrets

1. Pay attention to behaviors as indicators of culture. Seek to understand the rationale or values behind them.

2. Don't underestimate the power of culture, its importance to success, and its prominence in the failure to change or to ultimately achieve the vision, goals, and strategy.

3. Don't delegate the shaping of culture.

4. Politically appointed public sector executives must be realistic about what you can change given your relatively short tenure as executive.

Chapter Seven Exercise

Travel to a non-English-speaking country or a different part of your own country and keep a notebook. Jot down observed behaviors and identify cultural cues. This kind of practice in interpreting culture in new environments will sharpen your skills.

Chapter Eight

$\Big\{$ # TALK TO ME! $\Big\}$

$\mathcal{A}$s touched on briefly in Chapter Seven, how people communicate within an organization or a business is part of the institutional or corporate culture. In this chapter, we will delve more deeply into the subject of communication.

When you move into an executive position, if you don't already know how people in the organization communicate, it is important to observe and learn the preferred methods quickly. For instance, is highly important information communicated differently than routine information? Do people communicate via email, over the phone, face-to-face, instant message or text, over meals, through speeches, at the beginning of unit meetings, in large or small groups, sequentially, or in parallel fashion? As you observe communications, it's important to understand and distinguish the different methods employed for varied situations and leverage them when you begin communicating. Though it may sound counterintuitive, resist the urge to change the established communication methods initially. Begin by understanding the communication culture. Once you've established a degree of trust that ensures acceptance, you can bring in your own style. Let's start by looking at communications and a communications strategy.

What to Communicate

Executives must be deliberate in their communications. You should focus communications on the vision, strategy, change agenda, and how decisions are made as well as your team's successes.

Communicate the Vision and Strategy

Communication is a large part of your job as an executive, but just what are you communicating and to whom? First, you need to communicate to your core stakeholders inside and outside the organization or company. As discussed in Chapter Two, there are a number of external stakeholders who influence the environment in which you operate. These include competitors, cooperators, and collaborators in the value or supply chain; political actors whose actions shape your legal and regulatory environment; the board of directors; customers; shareholders; the public (especially if you are in a government institution); and the media. Internal stakeholders are just as numerous and important. They include your C-suite team; your executive staff; roughly the top 10% in the company or organization; divisions and groupings within the company that are organized functionally, geographically, or socially; and staff at the edge of the enterprise. When you put specific names in these categories, the list will quickly grow quite long, and you'll see why so much of your time is spent communicating and why so much of your time is spent outside of the company or organization.

Who needs to know your vision and strategy? The answer is simple: almost everyone. As you put your list together, ask yourself: Which other companies rely on your company's services or products? Who else is in the value chain? Why is it important for them to know your vision and strategy? What reaction do you expect to elicit from them? Are you looking for them to change their organization or company, their policies, or their attitude or mindset? From this list, you can quickly see that the size of the audience you will address and hopefully influence matters, as does the medium of communication.

Communicate the Change Agenda

As discussed in Chapter Six, as an executive, it is your job to make the business case for change and then sell it to everyone. Your sales pitch should be tailored to the stakeholder group that you are addressing. Your communication should incorporate their concerns, in general, and how the change will affect them, specifically. For example, how you communicate the business case for change to the board will be different from the sales pitch you give to new employees, the finance department, or the policy unit. How you communicate to a competitor will different from a potential collaborator.

Communicate How Decisions Will Be Made

It's important to communicate internally which decisions you will make as the executive leader, and which decisions will be made by others. The most consequential decisions, the most complex issues where uncertainty, risk, and ambiguity are omnipresent, should be reserved for the executive leader. This will be discussed more in Chapter Nine, but in a nutshell, decisions that are less complex, less risky, and have less ambiguity will naturally filter down through the organization or company corresponding to the level of responsibility, experience, and skill needed to make them. However, there are some decisions you must make, and you should inform staff how you will make them. These decisions usually entail gathering input from a group that you have established to research the issues and make recommendations. You establish this group, and then communicate the timing of the decision, rationale, and the process for examining issues, facts, and arguments. Regardless of whether you employ a consensus, a devil's advocate, a finding-the-truth, or a point-counterpoint style, it is important for you to describe the process when you first set up the group. Name the members of the team and their roles, give them the parameters, and give provide them with instructions and a deadline. You have to set this up. You cannot delegate it to anyone else.

Communicate Celebrations of Success

Celebrate when you reach success at any level. This is essential, because it sends a message about what is important to you and to the institution. Recognizing staff's successes helps build momentum and motivates team members to strive for more success. More than once a year, incremental wins should be recognized, especially in the initial stages of implementing change before the bigger impacts can be seen. Most people appreciate the personal attention that comes from being recognized by their boss. Recognition is a powerful motivating force, especially for those who strive for high standards of excellence.

Allowing people to own successes creates more loyal followers, and contrary to popular belief, ownership is not a limited commodity. It is counterintuitive, perhaps, to be broad and inclusive in recognizing success. You may believe that you will lose credibility in doing so, but you won't. With achievement recognition, employees and stakeholders feel a sense of pride in a job well done, which will be reciprocated back to you in the form of greater loyalty, support, and trust. Based on these, you can implement an even more ambitious agenda. It's a cyclical benefit that builds upon itself. In this respect, this is one of those counterintuitive secrets that not every executive knows, but those who do are bound for great success. So go ahead and recognize even the smallest actors. Watch what happens. You will be stronger for it, and you will have a more loyal following that creates even better outcomes.

Share the Credit

Years ago in India as the Director of USAID, I met with a handful of fellow senior officers to brief Jack Lew, then Deputy Secretary of State on a host of topics. Some I was quite conversant in and others I knew relatively little about given my brief tenure in India to that point. There was a discussion about issues of inequality and gender bias in the country. Uzra Zeya, then Minister Counselor Political Counselor in the Embassy spoke eloquently about the issue. She was characteristically poised and articulate. At the end of her five-minute response to Lew's question, she made a statement that basically gave me credit I felt I didn't deserve. She was very generous to include me in her examples of success. That small gesture, that nod of recognition, immediately caused me to throw my support her way. I had always admired her intelligence and confident demeanor, but when she gave me ownership of a relatively minor success in her report to the big boss, I felt like it was a kind and selfless gesture. I responded with loyalty and more support for her. I looked for ways to help further her agenda and struck up a friendship with her. This is a small example of what can happen when you allow others to own success.

How to Communicate

Executives must be deliberate not only in the content of their message but how they communicate. This begins with having a clear message and includes having an explicit strategy and plan for delivery, choosing the best messenger as well as choosing the means of communicating. The choice of the venue and the means of delivery are important components of how the message is delivered.

A Clear Message

Executive leaders must be specific about their message. They must define the message and communicate with clarity. They must know what action or change they desire to achieve through communication. Their communication must be planned and purposeful. Differentiate the key message to the group you are addressing. Speak to their position and their concerns. Simplicity is always a good idea.

A Communication Strategy and Plan

What is communication? Simply put, communication is an explicit and intentional message to an intended audience for a specific objective. Sometimes the objective is simply to make the audience aware, and other times, it's to elicit a behavior. The communication strategy, then, is the executive's plan for delivering the message to the audience in a way that elicits the desired response. There are many elements of a communication strategy. There is the messenger. There is the means, including both visual (written word) and auditory (spoken word) mediums. Communication can be one-on-one, to a small group, or to many people. There is one-way communication and interactive communication. There are degrees of message control that can be exerted. Which of these you use, when you use them, and how much you use them are all part of your communication strategy and plan.

Choose the Right Messenger

The designated messenger can be as important as the communicative content. A message from the President of the United States will carry more weight than one from the Secretary of Labor, and communication from the CEO will be more significant than that from one of many vice presidents. Pop stars, professional athletes, ministers, and clergymen can be very effective messengers to the right target group. Women may be more appropriate than men in some communicative circumstances, and vice versa. Sometimes members in the same social circles make the best messenger for getting the message across. In some cases you are the best messenger, and in others you are not. It depends on the target group and the action expected from the message.

Deliberate Ways and Means

The means of delivering a message includes the venue, the medium, and even word choice and tone. How will you address your audiences? Will you use mass media or face-to-face communication or something in between? Video clips or email? Newsletter or personal letter? Will you give a speech or have small group meetings in the cafeteria? Your choice of communication means is critical to getting your message to your intended audience with the intended impact. The medium you use to convey your message should be suited to the objective you are hoping to achieve. Whether you communicate via town hall meetings, the annual report to the board, television, radio, emails, face-to-face, or one-on-one depends on the intended target audience and objectives you hope to achieve.

Handle the Delivery with Care

When speaking to an audience, be sure to love the Ts and the Fs equally. What does this mean? People have preferred ways of interacting with the world. I distinguish between what I call the Ts and Fs. Ts are the Thinkers: they like big concepts and think and speak in those terms. They like words like "strategic," "logical," "results," "sequential," and "objectives." The Fs, roughly the other half of the world, are the Feelers, attuned to emotions. They prefer words like "passion," "compassion," "love," "harmony," and "enthusiasm." I've found that when giving a speech or any major communication, it is important to connect equally with the Ts and the Fs in the audience. If you are a T, using F words won't be your preference, but you need to use them to connect with the audience members who view the world through the F lens. The same is true if you are an F; use T words. You need to do this to connect with the audience and gain their trust, which by now you know that you must have if they are going to receive your message.

Executives who don't relate to the "other half" lose a huge portion of their audience. We've all listened to speeches by this type of executive. Many in the audience sit and nod their heads as if they understand, but in reality, they aren't listening or digesting the message. Executives who are aware of the differences between Ts and Fs however, and make it a point to use their language and speak using words they understand, will successfully relate to them, and they will listen to what you have to say.

Leverage Neuroscience When Communicating

The field of neuroscience is advancing opportunities to improve the way we lead and communicate. It explains how the human body reacts physically, emotionally, and cognitively to information. Neuroscience helps us understand how the brain impacts behavior and cognitive capacity. This information can be extremely helpful in our decision-making processes, in how we collaborate and build relationships, and in how we facilitate change. It is highly useful for enhancing communications so that the messages can be heard and digested by the recipients.

Interestingly, it has been shown that the brain changes with insights, and with practice it can develop new circuitry. Functional MRIs indicate that with an insight—the "aha" learning moment where we connect the dots or see an issue or a problem from a new perspective—the brain actually changes. These changes are permanent: it never goes back to the way it was before the learning moment. We remember insights because they are connected to emotions. So when communicating, especially one-on-one, it is important to have the recipient in a "ready-to-receive" mode, i.e., in a relaxed, nonthreatened state.

How do you put the recipient in a relaxed state or mood? According to David Rock's model[27], you want to reduce the stress caused by the five categories of stress generators. When stressed, the brain becomes less able to think clearly. This means as you engage staff, you want to take care not to create undo angst with statements that could unintentionally generate stress.

To avoid stress and have the clearest brain, best positioned to receive input, digest, think, and decide, keep the following in mind when communicating.

1. *Status threatened:* This relates to how you perceive yourself relative to others. For instance, we will fight a label if we think it is wrong whether that label is expressed or implied. When working in an interagency environment or with divisions across the company, it is important that you don't demean the status, authority, rank, or expertise of those you hope to influence.

2. *Certainty:* Your brain likes certainty; you are calmer when you know what to anticipate and there are no surprises. Clarity goes a long way toward reducing stress.

3. *Autonomy:* You covet your independence. You don't like to be told what to do and when to do it; you don't like to have to ask for permission or get approval for actions. To the extent one's independence is threatened, it creates stress.

4. *Relatedness:* The perceptions of people you don't know or who are of questionable allegiance creates stress. You are not likely to readily take in information from someone you don't know or with whom you have no relationship.

5. *Fairness:* How equal are we? If the perception is of unfairness, it increases stress.

The implications of these emerging applications from neuroscience are striking. A skilled communicator is able to choose her words wisely to avoid unintended threatening statement and heighten the likelihood that intended messages are conveyed.

First Observe, Then Change

In one organization, the new executive director imposed his communication style from day one without regard for the established culture. It had such negative consequences that, ultimately, his ability to implement the change agenda was severely limited. Traditionally, the directors in this company had met annually with each of his executive corps—his top 10%, his generals. It was a meeting valued by both parties. In addition, it was symbolically important and sent a message to subordinates and stakeholders about the cohesion of the organization. The new director did not hold these meetings. He stopped them without explanation or rationale. As a result, he lost the trust of his leaders along with their insight and knowledge. The executive corps felt demeaned. The executive was left scratching his head, wondering why the executive corps leadership team was hesitating to step up and embrace his agenda. Lesson learned! Don't try to change the way a culture communicates, at least until you've had time to assess and observe the established culture and communicate the changes you will make, along with your rationale for making them.

Speaking Volumes

Contrary to popular belief and somewhat counterintuitively, listening is a powerful form of active communication. Learning to be a good listener and adjusting the volume of your delivery to the person or situation will heighten the chances that your message will be received. As an executive, you should listen to your staff like you were listening to your baby's first words. Listen for tone and mood. Listen to what they are not saying. Listen to what their behavior is saying nonverbally. All of these will help you interpret the real messages they are communicating to you and, in turn, will help you understand how to communicate to them in ways that are meaningful to them.

Listening also generates trust. Here's how. Ask a question of someone you just met, and then listen closely to the response. Repeat the response back to her. This small gesture generates trust. I watched Olivier Carduner, the former mission director in Senegal, do this as a matter of practice. It led the people he spoke with to feel understood, which resulted in them feeling more comfortable sharing information and insight. Key for engendering trust and making a lasting and positive impression on others, listening is also an extremely valuable tool to gain insight and information to which you might not otherwise have access.

By virtue of your executive position, your voice is already amplified. For this reason, you don't need to talk loudly. In fact, your every move is amplified and staff will read meaning into everything you say and do, as well as everything you don't say or don't do. So, be strategic in your use of communication, both verbal and nonverbal. Know what you need to communicate, to whom, and the best medium to reach them.

"Actions speak louder than words." Consistency between actions and words will help to increase the volume of your message. How you conduct yourself when no one is looking, within your inner circle and in the larger group, shouldn't vary. People, especially subordinates, will pick up on any discrepancy and this will erode your credibility. Without credibility, you cannot lead effectively. Maintain congruence between your actions and your words and remember that nonverbal communication carries a message too.

Message Control and the Power of Variation

Messages have to be repeated many times before they are digested, understood, and acted upon. Scientific research on communication for behavior change has established that messages must be repeated again and again before anyone will willingly attempt the objective or behavior intended. What does this mean in terms of workplace priorities or in terms of the time you allocate for communicating with stakeholders or your senior staff? It means that, as an executive, you will spend a lot of time communicating. For this reason, use technology as the catalyst for delivering your message, as appropriate. Technology has opened the door to new approaches to communication. The principles of communication remain unchanged. The risk, however, is higher when one moves away from controlled messaging, but the chance of having a larger impact is also higher. Loosening control of the messaging allows communication to move in both directions, in fact, in all directions.

Loosening control of your messaging sounds counterintuitive, and it is. Instead of repeating the same message with new media channels, this kind of "now media" requires only that you maintain a primary theme or point, while allowing for variance in medium, messaging, and messenger. Experiment. Instead of one core message with identical wording that everyone recites verbatim or the daily talking points sent out from headquarters, this new approach allows you to vary the message as long as you stay focused on your theme. In return, you receive the potential benefit from the power of variation. By allowing your staff to use new words, their own words, by using pop culture words or art, and allowing the message to be transmitted via text, video, social media post, Instagram, and/or tweet, you have empowered those at the edge of the enterprise. "Now media" can reach many more people and might garner broader consideration than you ever imagined by capturing national or even global attention. So, lay out the themes, let go, and see what happens.

I can hear you saying, "What? Are you crazy? Loosen the reigns of the communication messaging and media?" Again, it is counterintuitive, but the days of one-way and controlled models of communication are gone. You need to go into this with your eyes open. There will be failures; that is certain. Plan for them and raise your risk tolerance levels. If you expect nine out of ten to fail, then you won't be surprised when the tenth goes viral with tremendous impact, it will have been well worth the risk.

Let me give you an example of an innovative public-sector communications program that proved particularly effective. Remember my tour in Peru? I was the director of the development component of the

U.S. counternarcotics program. Our aim was to reduce the amount of coca produced in the hinterlands of the Peruvian coca growing valleys. We used communication to raise awareness, to change what people knew and how they felt about coca, as a precursor to changing behaviors. We began by studying how people communicated a variety of messages and where they communicated what kind of information. Then we mimicked their communication means. We gathered and used data to inform the citizenry and the national public debate around producing coca. We honored cultural values and communicated in ways appropriate to Peruvian culture. We engaged stakeholders from university settings and politics, human rights workers and environmentalists, health activists and youth groups, to clergy and government officials, including the U. S. Congress and policymakers in the executive branch. We used TV and radio, both national and local, to disseminate information via news outlets, to host talk shows and debates, contests, songs, plot lines in soap operas, and commercial advertisements. We varied the message within a broad theme and we encouraged all of our stakeholders to engage publicly. We loosened message control and others projected the message in ways important to them. The end result of that year-long communication effort was measured change in national public opinion, a better informed citizenry, and a political body mobilized to take action.

We had a lot of fun working on that program. Our team and the Foreign Service and Peruvian teams worked very hard. Together it made for an incredibly rewarding environment that kept building on itself. Success breeds success.[28]

Measurement

A sure way to get your message across is to communicate clearly and with frequency. Most executives believe they do this, priding themselves on being as clear as a high-definition television with a sharply focused picture. Yet they collect no data to know with certainty whether their message is received and understood. In fact, lack of communication is one of the top concerns about executives heard from their subordinates. In order to deliver a clear message, first develop and test its clarity. Ask your audience to repeat back what they heard and understood. You may be surprised by their responses. Inevitably, there will be room for improving the message.

Roger That!

If you don't measure the response to your communication, how do you know if the intended message has been received? In the military, a "Roger that!" over the handheld radio is a clear and consistent way of indicating that a message has been received. As an executive, it behooves you to create your own "Roger that!" signal. Some executives have a habit of simply asking for a summary or next steps or requesting that the recipient parrot the message. It is not important what your "Roger that!" is, but it is important to have one.

Enough Already!

How do you know when to stop communicating to a particular group? How much should you communicate and how often should you repeat the message? Surprisingly, most executives do not communicate enough. They repeat their message, get sick of it, and then stop, believing everyone has heard it. The truth is that most people haven't digested the message yet. They may have heard it, but they have not internalized it. As an executive, you must repeat the message over and over again in different ways and in different venues. Stop only when you begin to hear the intended audiences, the receivers, reiterate your message. That is your "Roger that!" Only then will you know that the message is understood and will be remembered. Most executives, despite the "amplification" of their voices because of their leadership position, find that they must repeat any message at least eight times before it begins to sink in and they start to hear it repeated back. Choosing your words wisely and tailoring messages can accelerate this process, as can a solid trust foundation.

Another thing you can do to reinforce your message is use a near-immediate reward. It doesn't have to be monetary. It can be something as simple as inviting employees to a meeting they are not usually invited to or giving them recognition in a weekly internal news blog or email. For example, as soon as staff members begin to take action consistent with the message, step in and publicly recognize that behavior. Actions speak louder than words and rewards are loud actions, sending a clear message about expectations.

Measuring the effectiveness of your communication strategy is important in determining if your strategy is working. Clarity about what you are communicating and why will help you know whether the communication is having its intended impact. Survey instruments and behavior measurements are the most direct ways to determine if messages are being heard, understood, and acted upon. Invest resources in measuring the effectiveness of your communications.

Your communication strategy should be the savvy combination of message, messenger, and means to reach a target group with the frequency and timing that will be digested and acted upon. This implies, of course, that you know the behaviors or actions you want to elicit and why. To gauge effectiveness, you will want to measure the impact of the messenger, media, and message on each target group. Table 8.1 offers a way to plan and track your communication efforts to ensure targeted impact is achieved.

Table 8.1: Communication Tracking Chart			
Message to Convey	Messenger	Ways and Means of Delivery	Measure of the Impact
Succinct, single idea, reason, etc.	Person, symbols, relationships	TV, radio, email speeches, webinar, film, etc.	Knowledge, attitude, behavior
EXAMPLE	EXAMPLE	EXAMPLE	EXAMPLE

Summary

Communication is a large part of an executive's job, and how people communicate within an organization is a huge part of the culture. A skilled communicator is someone who can tap into the organization's culture, draw on the latest neuroscientific findings to differentiate messages to target audiences, listen empathetically, and convey information with clarity and the right frequency. The executive who is strategic in conveying messages and does so with authenticity and vulnerability will have the trust of her people and her messages will be heard and understood.

Chapter Eight Secrets

1. Understand and leverage existing communication channels.

2. Differentiate the message. Know what you need to communicate to whom and why.

3. Listening is a trust builder and an extremely powerful form of communication. When in doubt, listen.

4. When you speak, know your audience. Connect to the Ts (Thinkers) and Fs (Feelers) equally.

5. When communicating your message, repeat it until you hear the employees at the edge of the enterprise say it. Only then do you know your message has gotten through.

6. Celebrate by giving credit broadly, genuinely, and generously to others.

7. Above all, communicate authentically and with vulnerability.

8. Measure the impact of your communications strategy and plan.

Chapter Eight Exercise

Review the headings of Table 8.1, the Communication Track Chart. Choose one important message you intend to convey. Use the Chart to reflect, identify and plan the essential elements of achieving your communication objectives.

Chapter Nine

{ ONLY THE WICKED PROBLEMS PLEASE }

Finally, you're the boss, so you get to decide everything you want, right? Wrong. In reality, you want to make as few decisions as necessary. This is another example of the counterintuitive nature of executive leadership. Your job is not to solve all the problems or provide all the answers. In fact, you only want to solve the problems and make the decisions that others cannot make. You want your C-suite and your directors making all the decisions they possibly can. If you are making their decisions, you are disempowering them and taking on the liability for being wrong. Making decisions for them, you zap their intellectual and creative energy. You might as well have robots implement your decisions.

So, loosen the reins. Allow subordinates to do their jobs, make decisions, and own their initiative. It is counterintuitive, but true, that when you loosen your grip, you actually gain tighter control. Your people become more loyal followers because you have allowed them the space to carry out their responsibilities. This will also help them develop as they learn how to make decisions of greater and greater importance. As an executive, this is the golden ticket!

Leaders who do not relinquish decision-making control very often fit into the category of "micromanager." As you will see in Chapter Thirteen, a lot of executives micromanage because they don't understand what their position encompasses. They continue to do their old jobs, making decisions and solving problems that launched them to the executive level. However, at the executive level, the decisions to be made are fundamentally different. As you can see from the discussion in the preceding chapters, how you use your time and the role you play as an executive are different. When it comes to decision making, the executive should make only the decisions that others cannot. She must also ensure that how decisions are made are appropriate to the nature of the problem.

In the military and academia, they talk about "wicked" problems. Wicked problems and decisions about these problems are reserved for the executive. These are the types of problems that are so complex that they mutate, and static solutions don't help. Wicked problems can have four or five dimensions where linear thinking may not work. They require cross-departmental solutions at a minimum, and often require that components from outside the company or organization to be brought to bear. Even after all this, there is often no "right" answer; sometimes there is not even a "good" answer. By their very nature, these problems change when you intervene by attempting to solve them. These are the thorny problems reserved for the executive. These "wicked" problems should not be delegated. Realistically, this category of problems or issues accounts for about five percent of all decisions.

Part of the decision-making system is delineating the process by which decisions will be made. As mentioned in Chapter Eight, it is critically important, regardless of whether it is the executive's decision or an institutional decision, to be transparent about how the decision will be made, including who has what authority and what the limits of that authority are.

If you have aligned your internal systems well, then, in theory, your people should be able to make most decisions with reason, purpose, and defined processes. If your staffing is aligned, then you are pulling ideas and potential solutions from a workforce that brings a diversity of experience, backgrounds, frames of reference, mental models, and expertise to shape the solutions.

Interpersonal Skills in Decision Making

One of the major differences between leaders at lower levels and executive leaders, especially great executives, is the depth of their interpersonal skills. T.O. Jacobs[29] was one of the first to point to the increasing importance of interpersonal skills as one ascends the chain of command. To be most effective, interpersonal skills, emotional intelligence, and the ability to analyze and project these attributes are increasingly important because so many of the responsibilities of an executive rely on the foundation of strong interpersonal skills. Without them, a leader's impact is diminished.

Interpersonal skills include such things as charm, charisma, and empathy. Self-awareness can enhance interpersonal skills. Such skills are useful in decision making, negotiating, building trust, communicating, influencing and persuading, developing relationships, and inspiring. In short, the successful implementation of executive functions relies upon the strength and depth of the executive's interpersonal skills. These skills are referred to as "soft skills," but do not make the mistake of thinking they are subordinate to cognitive skills. Interpersonal skills play a catalytic role in the functions of executive leadership.

Interpersonal skills and emotional intelligence (EI) help us understand the feelings, attitudes, motivation, and behaviors of others. EI is the ability to interpret emotions with a degree of accuracy whether they are in ourselves or others, both as individuals and in groups. Daniel

Goleman, who coined the term, says that EI includes four domains of self-awareness, self-management, social awareness and relationship management.[30] Goleman notes that that, "Great leadership works through the emotions.[31]" Recognizing the power of emotions, great leaders know that emotions are contagious. They are not owned by anyone and no monetary value is associated with them. Yet the ability to interpret the emotions of another or the collective emotional center of a group—its "heart," so to speak—is a powerful skill.

The link between EI and great leadership is direct and fairly obvious. For instance, predicting and understanding your people's emotional reactions to a decision you might make, which can help mitigate negative consequences, is a beneficial skill to have. EI can help you understand that the position someone takes on an issue can be a reflection of a host of emotionally laden content, not just the issue at hand. If you have the ability to dig beneath the surface and understand the emotional undercurrents when a potentially destructive conflict arises, it will be extremely helpful in managing the conflict.

Finally, leaders with high EI know themselves, including how they are perceived by others and what their triggers are and why. This could be called "maturity," but whatever you call it, it is particularly helpful in executive leadership. This is more than the ability to see underlying emotions and understand the role they play in relationships, decisions, communications, and so on. EI is the ability to make decisions and take actions that promote the growth and forward movement of your organization or company and your people.

Structure the Decision-Making Authority and Process

Focusing at the systems level and solving problems that focus on how internal and external systems relate, you'll begin to understand multiple systems. Then you can think about and promote synergy among those systems toward the end of greater competitiveness for your company or greater effectiveness for your organization. That is the value added that executives bring to the job. For example, at a higher level you should be able to establish two fundamental parameters of decision making: 1) What level of authority you are reserving for yourself in the decision? 2) If you are establishing a team to tackle the problem, what level of authority does your designated team leader have? Victor Vroom initially put forward a hierarchy for guiding decision making process selection depending on the complexity of the problem and the importance of acceptance of the decision.[32] Vroom's hierarchy helps to determine what authority is delegated and what authority is retained by the executive based on the situation, the type of decision, and the nature of the problem. This kind of delineation may be helpful as you apply their model to your decision-making system.

- *Level I* is a traditional decision style. The leader makes decisions without consulting others, based on the information she has at hand. This is commonly known as "relying on gut instinct." In most cases, for tactical problems and day-to-day decisions, this is a useful approach.

- *Level II* is where the executive explicitly seeks input. This is commonly done in one-on-one meetings or routine meetings with senior staff. You ask—they answer. In all likelihood, you get what you ask for because you haven't given them any time to think about the intent behind your question, nor have they had any time to reflect and present a cohesive, thoughtful response. The subordinates have limited input.

- *Level III* is similar to Level II, except the number of subordinates who explicitly provide input is expanded but they are not brought together to reflect as a group. Staff have a better understanding of the problem and have time to think, prepare, and share their perspectives. The executive isn't compelled to use their input.

- *Level IV* builds on Level III, with the input of subordinates shared and perhaps generated in a group. The executive is not compelled to use their input. The traditional board of directors is an example of this level, as are the many established Executive Branch Councils at the federal level.

- *Level V* is a delegation of authority to the group itself, based on their shared analysis and ideas. The executive can be part of the group. Together, they evaluate and reach a consensus decision. In this case, the executive may act as a facilitator in reaching a group decision.

Some people wonder whether Level V decision making exists in practice. The U.S. President would never delegate decisions of consequence; the public wouldn't allow him to do so. On the other hand, the North Atlantic Treaty Organization (NATO) makes all of its decisions by consensus. NATO's reason for existing is to guarantee the freedom of all 28 member states. You can imagine the amount of discussion and level of constant consultation on issues important to the organization. Although Level V is the highest, there is no implication that it is "best" or even "better" than the previous levels.

Gut Instincts are Falliable

The executive gets into trouble when he uses his "gut instinct" to solve more complex problems where the environmental factors are not similar to past situations. Recent findings in neuroscience and the study of decision making bear mentioning here. Andrew Campbell and Jo Whitehead note, "The latest findings in decision neuroscience suggest that our judgments are initiated by the unconscious weighing of emotional tags associated with our memories rather than by the conscious weighing of rational pros and cons: we start to feel something—often before we are conscious of having thought anything."[33] Gut instincts are fallible. Know when and when not to rely on them. Stay abreast of the research coming out of neuroscience. This body of knowledge is growing rapidly and there are real implications for not only how to make decisions, but how to lead as well.

It is easy to see the varying levels of both input and authority in Vroom's hierarchy. You can quickly see the pros and cons of each and discern that for some types of decisions Level I is most appropriate, and for issues or problems of increasing complexity and consequence, Level IV may be most appropriate. Level V is reserved for when buy-in to the decision is paramount.

The important point here is that all decisions are not and should not be made in the same manner. As the executive leader, it is your job to distinguish the issues and couple the most appropriate parameters of decision making with them. For instance, some issues would benefit from input from a group or team. There are inner-circle teams, groups of advisors, and the so-called "kitchen cabinet." There are ad hoc teams pulled together quickly for the purpose of providing input only. There are task forces and commissions focused on a specific issue. It is your job to establish the team, and you should choose the members with intent or purpose. You should make clear the parameters of the team, including the authority and the process of decision making.

There are a multitude of types and hybrids of processes for decision making. You will use what makes the most sense for you and for the particular issue with which you are faced. However, as an executive, it is important to communicate to your team the process for making decisions.

Yes, decision making is often a process. It isn't as straightforward as just making a decision. In the process, you can use one of Vroom's lower levels, but when you do so, the risk of being wrong is heightened as the complexity of the problem increases. As hard as it may be to spend the time, for problems or issues of consequence, you need broader input.

As you assemble the group, you'll want to select individuals for specific reasons. Perhaps you require certain expertise about a subject or a certain type of thinker—conceptual, creative, or nonlinear. Do you need someone with experience in other environments or countries? The point is to select individuals with intent or purpose and communicate your rationale, so people understand why they are on the team and what is expected of them.

Next, you'll want to set up parameters, which depend on the problem. First, look at the objective. Is everyone on board with it? If so, you have a number of options. If not, then you've got a negotiation on your hands.

Consensus Decision-Making Process

Let's assume everyone agrees on the objective. In such cases, a consensus decision-making process is usually preferred. Most people are familiar with it and know how to engage in it. Essentially, everyone in the group is equal, shares his or her ideas, and has ample opportunity to be heard. As part of sharing, each member puts forward his or her assumptions, facts, ideas, and conclusions. Each person openly discusses the merits of each idea. Everyone tries to agree on assumptions and facts as a first step. They then focus on putting forward to the executive the best option in the form of a recommendation. Every member of the group need not be in complete agreement with the conclusion, but every member is heard and his or her ideas are given consideration. Again, not everyone need agree, but everyone must be able to live with the conclusion or recommendation.

Typically in a group process, one person or a small minority of people take over. They run the meeting, don't fully consider everyone's ideas, and don't formally come to a set of agreed-upon assumptions and facts. As a result, their conclusion or recommendations are hastily made and do not have the full support of all group members. In my experience, it is often the more vocal, senior, and in-the-box thinker who drives the agenda and pushes to conclude rapidly. I have been in many meetings run by senior government officials. Though everyone theoretically has a chance to voice his or her position, there is little time spent building on each other's ideas or attempting to reach a real consensus. If a consensus is reached, there is little discussion of implications or thinking through second- or third-order consequences.

For example, an interagency group may agree on a policy, but how the Departments of Defense and State interpret it is not discussed.

Thinking through the implications of decisions and consequences is needed to ensure that the spirit of the decision is fully implemented. In the worst case, parts of the federal government are working at cross-purposes, and more commonly, one part may be unintentionally undermining another. In a meeting where everyone is pressed for time, reiteration of the conclusions and next steps are almost never articulated and one must wait for the formal meeting notes to clearly capture the conclusions of the meeting and "voice" dissent.

This can be avoided. Do yourself and your subordinates a favor by, from the time the team is formed, setting the parameters, being specific, and recognizing the importance of taking the time to follow the process to produce the best, most considered conclusion or recommendation.

Varying Frames of Reference

An ability to view issues, solutions, and information through multiple perspectives or varying frames of reference is an important executive skill. By multiple perspectives, I mean through a political frame of reference; a short- or long-term perspective; an individual or group perspective; an analyzed interests perspectives; or through symbolism, thought, or structural frames. Each of these allows you to see the same problem or solution in a different light. By changing frames of reference, you can enhance your understanding of the issue, which is very helpful given the complex issues you face as an executive. This also allows you to put your feet in the shoes of another person in the group or in those of a key stakeholder.

For example, executives must be able to view decisions and actions through a political frame of reference: both a big "P" political (as in Democrat and Republican) and a small "p" political (as in office power centers and dynamics). Small "p" political are the power bases and sources within your organization or company and external actors who have influence over obtaining your vision or strategy. One of those external actors or stakeholders is big "P" political or the political system that resolves conflicts and makes decisions about competing interests like the distribution of resources and societal problems. Competition for political power drives decision making in this frame of reference.

When you understand the opposing view's perspective, then not only do you gain new insights for solving complex problems, but you are more likely to be able to gain their support, for you can now convey solutions through their perspective. It is an extremely powerful tool to be able to use their framework to relate to them.

Making a decision by consensus is good for routine decisions that have some structure to them. Decisions that need more thought and consideration than simple intuition or experience may best be made using the consensus decision-making process. This process, if conducted according to parameters, has the benefit of higher levels of buy-in. Note that I said if conducted according to parameters. Gathering input from individual members of the group results in the added benefit of higher levels of satisfaction and higher levels of understanding of the thinking behind the decision. Even if your individual idea didn't get picked up, perhaps one of your assumptions or facts was accepted, or at a very minimum you were able to understand the better alternative assumptions or facts. The process creates ownership and shared liability. Typically, the result of the process is a better synthesis of a variety of points of view, positions, assumptions, facts, and potential solutions.

Other Types of Decision-Making Models

As the complexity of the problem or issue increases, you will want to employ other types of decision-making models. For example, assuming there is agreement on the objective, you can set up what I will call a "truth-seeking" group comprised of two groups that role play in order to get to the truth and find the best solution. This can work in the following ways, each being iterative in nature:

1. Split the group into two subgroups. Subgroup I defines assumptions, facts, and a solution or decision. Subgroup II does the same thing separately. Then bring the groups together and reconcile any

differences to put forward one conclusion or recommendation to the executive.

2. Split the group into two subgroups. Subgroup I defines the assumptions, facts, and a solution or decision. Subgroup II attempts to challenge Subgroup I by critically examining its assumptions, facts, and solutions or decision.

3. Split the group into two subgroups. Have each subgroup take opposing positions and generate assumptions, facts, and solutions or a decision recommendation. Bring the two subgroups together and generate one set of assumptions, facts, and conclusions.

You can establish your own parameters and structures, but those described above are particularly valuable for complex problems or problems where the boundaries are not discernible. Guard against concluding prematurely, because premature conclusions probably mean limits were placed on the generation of potential assumptions, facts, and solutions. Push your staff to be critical of each other's ideas and rationale. Encourage dissent, and give people permission to think critically. They may not be accustomed to doing so, but it is vital for coming up with the best solutions and decisions. In these cases, an executive would receive the results of the groups' deliberations as input to the executive's decision (Vroom's Level IV). These are just a few examples of how the executive establishes the parameters of the decision-making process.

Conflict Management in Decision Making

A word about conflict: Conflict is inevitable when you bring people together. It is human nature. When you establish a decision-making process designed to encourage people to disagree with and challenge each other, conflict will in all likelihood emerge. As the executive leader, it is important that you make sure that the conflict remains intellectual and civil. Convey to the group that conflict is not only inevitable but desired, because with the productive use of conflict, better decisions can be reached. Warn people against conflict that crosses into the personal realm. Not only will it have a negative impact on the deliberations of the group, it can also have a negative impact on implementation of the decision and future group interactions. (See Table 9.1 for indicators that conflict has grown personal and could be detrimental.)

Be vigilant in looking for signs that conflict is turning personal. At that point, intervene in the group deliberations. Examine, learn and reset the course and the team for success.

Table 9.1: Indicators that Conflict Is Personal and Potentially Destructive
1. People show anger and frustration.
2. Values are violated.
3. One or more group members withdraw.
4. Body language says, "You're stupid," "You don't matter," "You don't get it," "That isn't feasible," or "You're wasting my time."
5. Inappropriate language is used.
6. There is a lack of respect.
7. Voices are raised.
8. Individuals pick sides rather than critically examining statements that are put forward.
9. There is an absence of "listening to understand."
10. Members are tense, not relaxed.

Understanding the roots of conflict and raising the awareness of the group, as a whole can be a great way to exploit a "teaching moment." Starting with the fact that conflict is inevitable and leading people to understand the benefits of conflict will help in managing it. If you need to step in because the conflict is crossing into a destructive or counterproductive arena, you will want to follow the steps in Table 9.2 to reestablish team cohesion.

Table 9.2: Steps to Reestablish Team Cohesion
Clarify the expectations of the group.
Reestablish trust within the group.
Surface the issue.
Understand the issue and its emotional content.
Ask the group to come up with potential solutions.
Have the group choose a solution to implement (a rule or standard of operations).
Draw lessons from the episode with the group.

Note that the stress that conflict can create detracts from the clear and rigorous thinking you expect from your subordinates. That said, you don't want to get involved in every case where intellectual and productive conflict goes south. Rather, reserve your involvement to those cases of consequence where the conflict could have a lasting negative impact on your organization or company. Think before you step in. You also want to avoid becoming the "go to" person for conflict resolution. It is easy for conflict resolution to consume large amounts of your time. If and when you intervene, conduct the session in such a way that the participants learn and are left empowered to solve the next conflict without your intervention. And, believe me, there will be a next time.

As you can see, it takes a fair amount of maturity to use processes that generate conflict. Companies or organizations that are sophisticated and healthy enough to employ these processes when needed will be able to make the best decisions, i.e., those that lead to a sustained competitive edge and highly effective organizations. It is easy to understand why interpersonal skills are so important and having promising staff serve on these teams is a great training ground for their future leadership.

Negotiated Decisions

In this chapter, I have presented a number of decision-making processes. Thus far, however, they include processes that are most useful when there is agreement about the objective. What happens if there is not agreement about the basic objective or the ultimate goal? This is common and is termed a "negotiated decision." By definition, there are at least two parties to a negotiated decision. The decision is made by two people or groups, within two separate parts of an organization, or between entirely separate organizations. What one individual, group, or organization wants and views as the objective is not the same as what the other side wants. In those cases, you need to employ your negotiation skills, and remember that you want to be involved in only those decisions or negotiations that affect the vision, strategy, or major systems of the organization or company.

The negotiation process is similar to other Level IV decision making in that it is focused on the problem and not the people. It is an iterative process. There is a lot of back and forth to gain greater understanding of each other's position, what is at stake, and each party's willingness to assume risk.

You may establish a group to represent you and to conduct the negotiations. As with other decision-making processes, you set up the team with intent, assign roles, and establish parameters. Conflict can emerge and it is your job to manage it if it threatens the team's cohesiveness. It is important to differentiate long-term objectives from short-term objectives. Seek a solution that is acceptable in the short term without losing in the long term. Keep negotiations above board. Don't lose trust by some intentional or perceived underhandedness. Seek a principled negotiated solution or agreement that both sides can live with and one that is viewed as a win-win solution. By doing so, you will preserve your integrity and trustworthiness.

Ethical Decisions

As discussed previously, a key function of the executive is to make decisions of the most complex variety that others cannot make. Invariably, ethical dilemmas will be one such category of decision that will fall into your lap. These kinds of decisions are not easy. For example, perhaps the right answer isn't clear. Perhaps there are two right answers or no right answer. Maybe you find that options are in conflict with competing values. Such dilemmas include, for example, difficult decisions where fundamental issues of justice are pitted against options of mercy, the good of the individual versus the good of the community is at stake, or short- versus long-term benefits are traded off.

For instance, do you dismiss a 20-year veteran for recent poor performance or do you keep him while he battles cancer? Do you alter your construction plans to the tune of several million dollars in order to protect a nest of rare birds? Do you allow a project to continue because it is politically important or do you stop it because it is failing to meet performance standards? Do you enter a country to protect its people when the state is committing atrocities? Do you do so in every case or in just some cases? If so, which cases? Do you do what is best for the greatest number of people even if that means doing wrong by one or two? Do you follow your personal moral compass or the moral compass of the commons? Do you look at the direct impact or the second- or third-order consequences? These are among the toughest decisions you will make. They will make you lose sleep at night. In these cases, there is no "right" answer. How do you decide?

It is useful to have a framework for understanding and making these kinds of decisions. Rushworth Kidder offers a simple checklist that you may find helpful.[34] He suggests that before making a decision, you first recognize the issue, identify who is involved in it, and ensure that all the facts are collected. In the process of making the decision, he suggests running through scenarios looking for a "sweet spot" of reasoning that offers the most convincing rationale. Ethical decisions are reserved for the executive because of their complexity and range of "right" decisions.

Summary

In the decision-making process, people will be more likely to support your decision if they have had a chance to put forth their ideas and solutions, to be heard. Even if the final decision contradicts their arguments, they are more likely to support it because they've been heard and their arguments have been considered. If they have been treated fairly and with respect, they are far more likely to accept the decision and implement it.

Because most people feel uneasy and uncomfortable with conflict, it's seen as a negative. However, as noted in this chapter, in order to get the very best decisions, you need the very best input and that requires that you create an atmosphere to surface contrarian views—even extreme views. Diverse opinions, perspectives, and approaches should be highly valued when solving complex problems. The wide variety that comes from diversity in people, whether as a result of diverse backgrounds, upbringings, expertise, experience, agendas, incentives, values, political beliefs, or cultures, is the engine for creativity. And, the "out-of-the-box" thinking that is the result of such diversity can be extremely valuable, especially when tackling "wicked" problems.

So, you want diversity, but with it, conflict is inevitable. This is not a negative! In fact, conflict is good. Conflict is an indicator of potentially rich ideas and solutions. Your job, when managing conflict, is to set the tone and parameters and keep the objective at the forefront of everyone's minds. The example you set and the direction you take should be with the notion that conflict is good and should not be avoided but rather managed. As part of the parameters you set, lay out boundaries to be sure the presentation and critique of ideas remains on substance and not personal.

Making decisions that have significant consequences to the business or organization's vision or strategy is your job, and relinquishing authority for all other decisions is key to developing subordinates and winning loyalty of staff. Relinquish your authority for most decisions and structure decision-making processes so that the business or organization maximizes its talent and builds capacity. Ensure that the complexity of the problem drives the use of appropriate decision-making models. Step into decision-making processes selectively, and do so only when constructive and productive conflict moves into destructive or personal conflict. Especially in these cases, strong interpersonal skills are imperative. Remember that only the "wicked" problems, ethical issues, and formal negotiations are where you need to spend your decision-making time.

Chapter Nine Secrets

1. It is important as an executive that you loosen the reins. Allow subordinates to do their jobs, make decisions, and own their component parts.

2. Make only those decisions that others cannot make, and only ones of substantial consequence—those that affect position, strategy or major resources of the company or the organization. Reserve your energy for the most complex or "wicked" problems.

3. Be explicit about the type of problem/issue you face and compose an intentionally diverse group to review it. Then set parameters for the group to examine facts, arguments, and options for recommendations.

4. Diversity in people is a powerful resource. Conflict in decision making is inevitable. Understand and capitalize on diversity and conflict in decision making.

5. Examine, learn, and reset. Manage conflict that turns destructive or counter-productive and threatens cohesiveness. Reserve your involvement to cases of consequence or potential lasting negative impact.

Chapter Nine Exercise

Make a list of your biases. Be honest. What are your beliefs or values or experiences that may bias your decision making? Write them down. Think about how you will avoid these biases and hold yourself accountable in your personal decision-making process.

Chapter Ten

{ # YES, YOU CAN HAVE WORK-LIFE BALANCE! }

This chapter reveals the secrets of the seemingly elusive balance between your work priorities and ambition and your personal life and happiness. This is commonly referred to as work-life balance. As an executive, it is important that you spend time every day taking care of yourself. In Chapter One, I suggested that 5% of your time every work day should be focused on yourself. That is about 30 minutes a day to focus on no one else but you. Although counterintuitive, prioritizing relaxation and caring for yourself is part of your job. Take the time. Don't ask permission. Schedule the time and use it to take care of yourself. Successful executives are those who take care of themselves and understand the connection between caring for themselves and great leadership.

Taking Care of Yourself

Working long hours is detrimental to achieving the vision and goals of a company and organization. Again, it is counterintuitive, but working normal hours may have a positive effect on productivity and, as a result, may enhance your organization's competitiveness and effectiveness. Like so many things about executive leadership that are counterintuitive, working reasonable hours actually results in greater value added. It forces you to be more efficient in the use of your time, to prioritize, and to reserve time for nonwork activities that supplement your happiness.

Be Yourself

Unless someone tells you otherwise, you may believe that all great executives are cut from the same cloth. They aren't. In fact, pretending to be an "executive" can be off-putting to others and exhausting for you. We've all seen the new executive who has the perfectly coiffed hair, expensive suits, nice cars, says little in meetings, but seems to sit in judgment and enjoy making others shake in their boots. When he does speak, his language is formal and stiff. He doesn't joke or jest. He sits up straight and is all business, all the time. People walk on eggshells around him. If you are this executive, acting differently than you really are is not genuine and will quickly turn people off. They certainly won't trust you. It is exhausting to stay in character and be guarded for fear of exposing your weaknesses or secrets. And when you are exhausted, you become stressed.

It is a lot easier and more effective to simply be yourself. Embrace your strengths and weaknesses, hopes and fears, and triumphs and failures. If you accept yourself, so will your staff and your stakeholders. There is no established style or preferred mannerisms for executive leaders other than to be themselves. You will be more effective if you expose your whole self and through this vulnerability, you will gain the trust so essential to being a great leader. Bottom line is, if you do nothing else, be yourself.

Be Yourself

I never dreamed of becoming an executive until the first time I had a female supervisor who was completely authentic, Jennifer Windsor. I noticed distinct differences in the way she managed versus neraly all the previous supervisors I'd worked with. Jennifer was less formal in her speech. She was comfortable with herself and relaxed in her work environment. She smiled a lot. She joked with staff. She asked insightful questions. She cared about her work. Her style and manner were different from those of others. For the first time, I saw that I could be myself and relax. I could make mistakes and ask for help. I could give my opinion in my own words without being judged. Jennifer demanded the same rigor of thought and performance standards that every boss ever required. She was an incredibly effective executive who led the establishment of a global democracy and governance program at USAID. That experience was a real eye opener for me. For the first time, I could see myself in an executive position because I could see that it was okay to be myself. In fact, not only was it okay, it was more effective. As a midlevel staff, executive leadership looked inviting for the first time.

Relax

Putting yourself first, above other priorities, is important to ensuring your high productivity. Spend some time every day doing something that relaxes you. It can be a hobby, exercise, or pursuing an area of interest. What you choose to do doesn't matter so much as does taking the time to relax and do something you like. Some people cook or play bridge; some practice singing or acting. Others volunteer at their churches or take part in civic activities. Having a relaxing hobby or outside interest that brings you joy is critical to maintaining your productivity as an executive. You do insightful thinking in a relaxed state of mind, so balancing work and relaxation is conducive to good decision making.[35] And, because the decisions you make have serious consequences for your company or the organization, it is important to promote regular relaxation, whatever that might be. Also, you are the model for others to emulate. If you take time to take care of yourself, others will feel justified in doing the same.

Have you ever wondered why some of your best ideas come to you while you are taking a soothing shower or right before you fall asleep? Neuroscience has revealed how exposure to stress causes the rapid loss of prefrontal cortex cognitive abilities.[36] Think of the implications of this for the workplace! If you want your employees to make good decisions and generate great ideas, you want them in a relaxed state. Integrating relaxing activities into their day is one way to achieve this. Model this behavior for your staff and ensure systems are in place to support self-care throughout the enterprise. The entire company or organization will benefit.

It sounds counterintuitive: "Allow staff to relax on the job and they will be better performers, more productive, and more ingenious?" It is true for them and it is true for the executive. When looking at habits of highly successful people, Stephen Covey says they give priority to a period of time every day when they relax and renew.[37] He claims this is an essential habit that makes all the other habits of successful people possible.[38] They reserve and protect that time and no one schedules on top of it.

One way to relax is through exercise, which has many other benefits, as well. It is an investment that has long-term financial gains in terms of decreased medical expenditures and short-term benefits in increased energy and a sense of well-being. It demands exertion from your muscles, including your heart, and also relaxes them so that they can operate more efficiently. It helps with weight control and keeping your body toned.

Reading is another way to relax that has many benefits. Widening the breadth of your reading develops your conceptual capacity. The more diverse genres you read, the more you learn. Our military leaders, corporate executives, and other leaders often publish their reading lists.

What If?

Sometimes I wonder what would happen if every employee across the U.S. were allowed 30 minutes a day for exercise, reading, or a hobby, with pay. I suspect if we instituted such a policy, we would find that stress would be better managed, decisions would be of higher quality, innovation would spike, and employees would be more productive and happier. And perhaps, in the long-run, healthcare costs would be lowered. I believe this may just be the next advantage the U.S. needs to enhance our global competitive edge.

Spending a little time every day on something that relaxes you contributes to establishing and maintaining work-life balance, which is critically important to your success as an executive.

Work-Life Balance

When I was an officer on the brink of crossing the threshold to executive positions, my executive-level supervisor told me that at the Senior Foreign Service level (the executive level), I would need to be prepared because I would be on duty 24/7. She said that if I wasn't prepared for this time commitment at the lower leadership ranks, I would never make it to the executive level. She wanted me on-call whenever she needed me. She expected me to work on Sundays and to socialize with her during my "off" hours. She often requested that I include my spouse in these social/work events. As you can imagine, that was the last thing my spouse wanted to do, especially after he saw how the executive was unreasonably demanding of her staff. Work encroached on my personal life and my spouse resented it. I rejected the notion that I needed to be available 24/7 then and, after having served in executive positions, I continue to reject it.

I have come to the conclusion that this kind of "do-whatever-it-takes" attitude is destructive and counterproductive. Occasionally putting in extra hours because of extraordinary or unusual demands is one thing. It is quite another to be required to work long hours on a regular basis. It isn't healthy, and humans are not built nor conditioned for it. When we work in an overload capacity, we do not operate at full cognitive capacity and our thinking becomes impaired. We become stressed, and stress pushes us to the extremes of our personality preferences. High levels of stress will eventually result in bad decision making, as you'll see in the following story.

Watch for the Red Flags

Years ago, as a junior officer, I had a conversation with my boss about work-life balance. What I learned from him has served me well throughout much of my career. Dr. Jeff Harris was the head of a new unit in USAID called the AIDS Division, established in the late 1980s to prevent the spread of human immunodeficiency virus (HIV) and acquired immune deficiency syndrome (AIDS). Jeff was a young physician detailed from the Centers for Disease Control (CDC). Exceptionally bright, he graduated early from both high school and medical school. He had an incredible ability to see the big picture, understand the external environment, and set a vision. He took a small team and turned it into a unit that served as a catalyst for learning and experimenting with prevention methods early in the AIDS epidemic. He seemed to lead with such ease. He engaged external stakeholders from multiple arenas (including the medical research community, the political community, and neighborhood and community organizers from San Francisco) to learn as quickly as possible from each other and transmit the lessons learned to the developing world and back. He was a demanding leader who had little tolerance for anything short of excellence. He pushed us to excel. My work hours grew longer and longer in my attempt to meet Dr. Harris' standards and position myself for a promotion.

One afternoon, I asked him, "How do you know if you're working too much? How do you know if you're a workaholic?" "Watch for the red flag," he told me. "Listen to those around you. If your husband ever complains or makes comments about the hours you are working, then stop and listen to what he's saying."

I walked away thinking I hadn't heard anything yet, so I must be okay. But, my antennae were up and I did listen for that question, "Are you working late again?" from my husband or a comment from myself like, "I need to spend a couple hours on Sunday catching up for the beginning of the work week." Hearing yourself continually apologizing with, "Sorry, I'm late," is a sign, too. It means I had to work extra and as a result was late to a social event. These may not seem like red flags, but they are. If you do not stop and listen to your loved ones, colleagues, or yourself, you will probably regret it down the road. These red flags signal that your work life is encroaching on your personal life.

If you aren't sure yet whether you are exhibiting "workaholic" tendencies, run through the questions in the exercise below and reflect as you read the rest of the chapter.

Exercise 10.1: Workaholic Tendencies Worksheet

0 is never
1 is occasionally or one time per month
2 is sometimes or one time per week
3 is regularly or two or more times per week

_____ I work more than eight hours per day.

_____ I spend time over the weekend working to prepare for the upcoming week.

_____ I eat lunch at my desk.

_____ I miss family events or personal appointments to complete work.

_____ I arrive earlier to work than I am required to report.

_____ My partner or spouse comments on the amount of work I do or the amount of time I spend working.

_____ I think about work when I am not working.

_____ I go through my in-box or work papers at home.

_____ I miss dinner with my family due to work.

Total your points and use the rating guide to determine your vulnerability to workaholism.

Ratings

0-5...   *No issues, likely good work-life balance*
6-10...   *Mild, monitor your work habits*
11-20... *Red flag waving, pay attention and cut back*
21-30... *Danger, burnout likely*

Personal Alignment

Some people have so closely aligned their core personal values with their career lives that it is hard to see a division between their work and nonwork lives. An example that comes to mind is Dr. Helene Gayle, another young physician on loan from the CDC who led the HIV/AIDS unit of USAID. Helene's work and personal life seemed like one and the same. She had dinner parties that included people from her work life. She met with people from the political arena and they were her friends. She seemed so at peace, confident, and smart. When she did a round of television interviews, she needed next-to-no preparation because her work was her life. She had a genuine interest and loved to engage on the range of topics that were related to health. It was clear that helping people and health were her core values, which, in turn, were fully consistent with the requirements of her position. This alignment showed in the ease with which she conducted herself and the confidence with which she spoke. When you have a high degree of personal and professional values alignment, work-life balance is more easily attained.

Know Your Job

Knowing your job is the key factor in establishing and maintaining work-life balance. Once you know what your job is and what it is not (as discussed in previous chapters), you can set parameters for how you will spend your time. This kind of information shines a light on progress, trends, and lessons learned and can delineate course corrections. If you don't understand your job, you may feel like you need to do everything, meet with everyone, and know everything to do a good job. This is not the case. Being clear about what your job is and how you should spend your time will help you weed out the less important from the most important. (Notice everything is important!) As an executive, your job is to focus on the most important, the most consequential.

Leadership Readiness

Do you have the skills, experiences, and disposition to be an executive? I'll discuss this in greater detail in Chapter Twelve, but in general, you probably know if you have the mindset for, and are comfortable working in, the executive environment. If you do not, then you are likely to compensate with controlling behaviors, temper flare ups, or working long hours in an attempt to master your role or veil your fears and weaknesses. Working long hours is not sustainable. Something will give. I've seen it over and over again. When leaders work long hours for sustained periods of time, their health, family, marriage, or work performance (or a combination of all of these) suffers, and sometimes they face a life-altering crisis. Veiling your fears and weaknesses also doesn't work. It does not allow you to be vulnerable. Without vulnerability, you will not gain the trust needed nor the loyal followers needed to achieve your work goals.

Set Boundaries

How much you work is your choice. There are those who believe work-life balance is misguided. They argue that if you simply do what you love and love what you do, you will be happy, like Helene in the example earlier in this chapter. For Helene, work was fun, and the question of work-life balance never seemed to enter the conversation. Other people believe that work-life balance is simply unattainable in today's work environments with the technological advancements and resultant appetite for instant responses and solutions. For instance, many people can't let an unopened email from the boss sit. They respond immediately, and they find it impossible not to continually check emails or other channels of communication. They have not set communication boundaries.

We all know people who can't say "no." There are many reasons saying "no" is hard for them. They were never taught how to say it, or they may view saying no as a sign of weakness. They may be afraid that if they say "no" to a request, they are saying "no" to the next promotion or chance for advancement. They may not want to turn down a challenge. They may not even see "no" as an option, because they were never taught how to put themselves first–how to make their interests, happiness, and growth a priority. The people who can't say no are often the people who have a disproportionate amount of work. They may or may not complain about the workload. However, what happens is these people tend to have many more actions to complete and even if they work long hours, the quality is lower than what it would have been if they had fewer actions. Those who are likely to get promoted are those with the highest quality work and not those who have the largest quantity of work. Saying "no" and setting clear boundaries not only helps with establishing a balance, it also positions you better for promotions.

If you want work-life balance, find the courage to negotiate reasonable boundaries and timelines that allow you to do your very best. Become known for the quality of your work, not the quantity. This is notably harder at executive levels where the stakes are high and the career pyramid is narrow. However, for your good and the good of your organization or company, find the courage to have a conversation with your boss about the difference between the most important and the just important. You can't do everything. No one can. It may be counterintuitive, but give yourself permission to say, "Not only is work-life balance good for me and my family, it is good for me as the head of this organization or company." A more narrow scope can make you more successful. If you put your best efforts, your highest quality of work, and your best thinking into fewer, more important objectives, success and balance will come.

Better yet, ask yourself why you feel compelled to work late repeatedly or use the weekend to catch up. What is the cause of that demand? Is it your boss or is it you? If it is you, why are you doing this? Why do you feel like you need to work such long hours? Is there something you are afraid will happen if you don't work so many hours? Are you compensating for something? Maybe you don't feel skilled, smart, or organized enough to get your work done in the regular 40-hour work week hours. It is important that you think about the demands you are putting on yourself and ask why.

In my case, early in my career, I never felt quite smart enough or adequately trained. I felt I was supposed to know much more than I did. Putting in long hours, I felt I was compensating for this inadequacy. I realized later in my life that I was smart, experienced, and skilled enough. My career trajectory supports this notion. It was the voice inside my head that allowed self-doubt to drive my workload. I began to resent the need to work such long hours. My family hated it. My health suffered. I reduced my weekly exercise and put on weight. The stress grew. Finally, after a decade, I decided I wasn't happy and that the long hours were impacting my family, my staff, and me. So, I pulled back, but it wasn't easy.

Focus on the Few

Don't fall into what Marshall Goldsmith calls the "over commitment trap."[39] This is the trap of trying to do too many things, and as a result not doing any as well as you could. It leaves a less than satisfactory feeling in your gut and can have some potentially bad side effects, such as disappointed bosses and low quality work. In *Mojo*, Marshall notes that people who do three or four things well are not only happier and have more balance, but they tend to get promoted sooner than the "utility infielder" who takes everything that comes their way. Though the infielder is dependable and completes every task, they are so rushed that they don't do their best work. They meet deadlines and are given more work, often becoming the "go to guy/gal." Rarely do they take the time to produce their best work. As a result, they are left with an empty feeling that doesn't promote high self-esteem.

Wading into the Work-Life Debate: Yes, You Can!

The best defensive move you can take to guard against work-life imbalance is to know your job well. Know what it is and what it isn't. Know what is expected of you and what the boundaries are. Know the most important parts of your job and prioritize your time. Know that the job is dynamic and the more you do, the more will come to you. There probably aren't enough hours in a day to do absolutely everything you want to do and maintain balance, but you can get 95% there with a normal work schedule.

What is a normal schedule? I cringe when I hear of executives and leaders who make the same mistake I did by keeping incredibly long hours. Reading Anne Marie Slaughter's *Atlantic Monthly*[40] article on work-life balance, I gasped at the part about when meetings for the day ended, the writing work began. I gasped because I could completely relate to it. Personally, I worked all day and left the office about 6 or 7 p.m. I'd spend 30 minutes eating dinner before getting back to work until 10 or 11 at night. I suspected then, and now I know, that not only doesn't it have to be that way, but also, it shouldn't be that way.

If you are working through a stream of decision memos and reports after your workday ends, then something is wrong. Either too many things are coming to you for decisions or you are asking to make more decisions than necessary. If you are editing documents in the evenings, it makes me question, why? Is that for a document to have your initials or your signature on it, so that it reflects your personal work? Maybe something is out of alignment with the system that demands so many meetings and reports that it requires evening hours to maintain.

Every meeting and every document cannot be a value-add to the vision, goals, and strategy of your organization or company. And remember, your job is to focus on the vision, goals, and strategy. The rest is for others to do.

The fact that Dr. Slaughter couldn't find time during the week for personal errands is disturbing. Why couldn't she schedule time between 12 and 2 p.m. each day? When did she have time to reflect and think? Did she take time to develop her staff, her number one job as an executive? Reading the article, Dr. Slaughter began to take on the very characteristics and behaviors that support the status quo—the very same status quo she believes needs to change.

Over and over again I've seen and experienced in my own life, that there is a limit to how much people can work and maintain their effectiveness. Just like everyone needs different amounts of sleep, everyone has a different threshold for work before fatigue begins to set in and work becomes less efficient and effective. When you repeatedly exceed that threshold, your body feels the stress and it begins to take a toll in other areas of your life. Inevitably something gives, and either your work, you family life, and/or your health suffers. If you don't listen to the warning signs, you are likely to suffer a personal crisis somewhere along the road.

Ultimately these are the decisions you make for your own well-being. If you do not make them, they will be made for you. Take control and consciously decide the quality of life you want to have. You can have it all. The operative word here is "all" and how you define it. Success and happiness are very possible together as is a balance of work and life. You just need to know your job and yourself and ensure that the two are aligned. And you need to have the courage to follow a counterintuitive measure, narrowing scope to the most important objectives. Then you can have it all!

Partner Choice

Remember the question, "Do you want to dance?" Well, one "yes" response to that question led to one of the best career decisions I ever made. That dance lead to my marriage two-and-a-half years later. Even though I didn't know it at the time, marrying my husband, Ben, has had a significant impact on my ability to lead and advance my career. He has been instrumental in helping me excel and achieve career milestones. He was always by my side as I climbed the career ladder and forewent a career himself in order to support me in mine. That one decision, particularly for a woman, is a big factor in how well you are able to balance work and life. A spouse who shares household management, child rearing, and other family duties provides the level of support needed to devote quality time to the job. Having a supportive spouse can make work-life balance manageable. Yet, even with a supportive spouse, you still have to train yourself to listen for the signs that your work is spilling over in an unhealthy way into your personal life. Set your boundaries and commit to sticking to them.

Understand Neuroscience

If you want work-life balance, it will help immensely if you understand a bit of brain science. You do your best thinking and you are your most creative and innovative when you are in a relaxed state. In this state you can connect the dots. Solutions emerge and your conceptual framework becomes denser. You are able to learn. It's also important to know how your brain reacts to stress. For example, while under stress your decision-making is hampered, your thinking is less clear, and your reactions are sluggish. If you take the time to keep up with the practical findings of neuroscience research, you'll know the factors that elicit or produce the best thinking and the best leadership.

Summary

We've heard a lot about work-life balance, but who actually practices it? Great leaders do. Taking care of yourself and prioritizing yourself is critically important to executive leadership. Being yourself, making relaxing a priority, getting regular exercise, and maintaining a balance between work life and personal life are the self-care elements found in truly great leaders. It's not easy and it can take some practice, but understanding what your job is and what it is not helps in achieving work-life balance as does ensuring that your personal values align with the company or organization you are leading. Staying abreast of neuroscience in leadership, setting clear boundaries, focusing on the few most important key objectives, and having a supportive partner are all secrets to achieving work-life balance. As an executive you can achieve career success and have a happy and fulfilling personal life.

Chapter Ten Secrets

1. Delegate as many tasks as possible and trust your staff to perform.

2. Avoid encroaching on the duties, functions, or responsibilities of subordinates.

3. Above all else, be yourself.

4. Schedule time every day to relax and protect that time.

5. Watch for the warning signs of work-life imbalance.

6. Pursue executive positions that align with your personal values.

7. Be prepared with the right skills, experiences, and disposition to be an executive.

8. Know your job and the boundaries of your responsibilities.

9. Choose a supportive partner who will put equal importance on your career ambitions as on his or her own.

10. Negotiate with your supervisor the "critical" from the "important" work or objectives.

11. Become known for the quality of your work rather than the quantity.

12. Stay abreast of research coming from neuroscience leadership.

Chapter Ten Exercise

If you haven't yet completed the Workaholic Tendencies Worksheet, do so. After determining your rating, write down three actions you can take immediately to ensure a greater work-life balance (refer to Chapter Ten Secrets) and track it until you achieve it.

Chapter Eleven

REFLECT, LEARN, GROW!

I n previous chapters, I have discussed the importance of setting aside time every day to reflect, think, and learn. At least 5% of your time should be spent on these activities. As counterintuitive as it may seem, setting aside time each day to consciously reflect is key to being a great leader. Yes, every day, even, and especially, when a crisis is erupting, you need to continue your daily reflection time. Even when your "to do" list is full of immediate, urgent actions, you should set aside time to reflect. Even when you are up against hard deadlines, it is important to reflect regularly. During reflection is when you focus on what you are learning and how you will proceed in your development as a leader. This is the time for your personal growth as an executive. Schedule time for reflection every day and honor its importance by coveting the time. It may take some getting used to, but the rewards will quickly become obvious.

Reflection time is a fundamental source of learning because re-flection is the kind of undisturbed, deep thinking that promotes insight or cognitive breakthroughs. It is when you review your actions and in-teractions both personally and professionally that you spot patterns and identify lessons. It is when you review your progress towards personal and professional goals. It is a time to integrate what you are learning (both cognitively and emotionally), the events taking place in your life and in the organization, and the feedback you've received from your peers, direct reports, family, and friends. It is when you consider what is good, what could change, and what might be your next steps, be they for the next hour, the next day, or possibly longer.

No one stops learning or receiving new information, so it is im-portant to take the time to understand what new information is coming to you each day and how it plays into what you already know. Like any skill, it takes time and practice to make reflection a habit and to get the most out of it. Research shows that the brain changes as a function of where the individual puts their focus. Reflection that focuses regularly on becoming a better leader, or any specialty, will result in physiological changes in the brain itself indicating learning and new perspectives.[41]

Because your growth as a leader is incremental, you can't short-cut or skip the stages of cognitive or emotional development. Addition-ally, cognitive development does not necessarily expand in parallel with emotional development, but you need both to carry out the functions of your job.

There are things that you can do to accelerate the pace of cogni-tive and emotional learning. Habitual, regular reflection is one of these. An executive must develop habits that sharpen and improve her skills step by step.

It has been my experience that adults learn when they are ready to learn, i.e., when they face a problem and need answers or help. They need to know how others have faced similar issues. They need to un-derstand what they did wrong or how they were blindsided. They want to create a different future, perhaps one with greater work-life balance or respect. This is when they are primed for reflection. By setting aside time each day to reflect, you carve out time to learn and develop both cognitively and emotionally, and ensure that you don't miss an opportunity to grow.

Making the Time

How do you find the time in your already full schedule to reflect, think, and learn? It starts with simply scheduling this time like you would schedule any other meeting. Call it "reflection' or "preparation time." Call it whatever you want, but schedule it and don't give it away. Don't allow your scheduler to postpone, move, or cancel it. Don't let other priorities encroach on this time. It is that important. Stop all incoming calls and turn off your cell phone. Close your door so that you won't be interrupted. If possible, don't sit at your desk. Instead pick another chair, one that faces a window that you can look out of. If your office isn't conducive to creating a quiet and uninterrupted environment where you can think, then go for a walk, go to the library, or go to a café where you aren't likely to run into anyone you know. Some people reflect habitually during their daily exercise routine. The where and how of it are less important than that you are alone in a place where you can clear your head and think uninterruptedly. Remember, as the leader, it is your job to reflect and do deep, quality, critical and creative thinking on behalf of the company and organization that you are leading.

You may not have an issue to deal with each day that requires deep reflection, but you'd be surprised how frequently you use this dedicated reflection time to think through an issue, to prepare your performance, or to analyze and synthesize seemingly disparate data points or indicators. You might use it to look for trends and patterns in your organization or company or to open the door to creative or counterintuitive solutions. During reflection, you turn off the intuitive thinking that is quick and reactive and based in your personal experience, and you allow yourself to deconstruct a problem and examine assumptions at a deep level. You can sharpen your skills when you set aside time daily to think both critically and creatively.

What else can you do with reflection time? You are free to think about anything you want! Use the time to consider how to approach external stakeholders or synthesize information you receive from them. Think through an internal alignment issue or about how best to promote staff development. Interpret observed behavior or your own behavior and feelings vis à vis others. For instance, what bothers you? What is it that causes this stress? What can you do to build trust? You may want to detangle a thorny issue that takes an extended period of concentration before you attend a meeting on the topic. Or you may use the time to focus on systemic issues to promote greater alignment. Personally, I often use the time to replay meetings or presentations to contemplate what went well and what could have gone better; there is always room for improvement. Some people journal during this time about their thoughts and feelings as an aid to creative and out-of-the-box thinking. They examine potential second- and third-order consequences and plan for them.

During reflection, you may want to think back over your day, week, and month. Look for patterns and trends in your behaviors and thoughts. Think about the future and how to bring forward lessons about individuals and groups, and about stakeholders' demands, perspectives, and offerings. This kind of reflection is critical to learning, to break-throughs in solving problems, to insights on relationship issues, and to improvements in your performance. It is a chance to dream, conceive, and create, to reflect on why and why not, to discover how to achieve a milestone or get your point through to a subordinate in a way that the subordinate can take action. The key to reflection is to schedule it daily and safeguard it. Most adults learn tremendously during this period of analysis and synthesis of information. And once you make reflection a habit, you'll wonder how you managed without it. Next, let's review some of the common ways executives learn.

Training

Executives must spend some of their time learning. The problem is that most people are trained in classroom or conference settings and then expected to translate the knowledge learned there into new skills and apply them back at the office, away from the classroom setting and trainers.

While companies and organizations rely on training for emerging leaders, high potentials, and rising talent, few provide classroom training for executives. The amount of training varies widely, but it is almost always insufficient or inadequate. For example, I received only five weeks of leadership training in my entire career and, of that, only one week was geared to the executive level. I was provided an executive coach and she was extremely valuable. The military provides multiples of five weeks of training for their equivalent high potentials and aspiring leaders; however, most executives will tell you they were not adequately prepared.

For instance, executives are expected to absorb a year's worth of important information crammed into a three-day workshop. Typically, such delivery of volumes of leadership training material over a relatively concentrated period of time is not conducive to the day-to-day application of the new material. The leader must learn, attempt, and adopt the new skills presented during the training in order to execute them on the job. If you're like most people, you will remember two or three key concepts from the training, regardless of its length. When you are back on the job, assuming the environment is conducive to attempting the new skills, you may try one or two of them. If you don't have immediate success, you'll likely file the knowledge away for another day or situation. Beyond that, participants in classroom trainings don't retain much information. They are so focused on the issues of the day that they can't adopt and master the skills they need to succeed. Classroom training is good way to introduce new concepts and tools, but it is insufficient as a sole means of learning.

Because there are very few courses for executives once they reach this level, and even if there were more training offered, they are often too busy to take the time to enhance their own development, great leaders use their personal reflection time to learn. And they don't stop there, but use other means to continue to learn and grow as well.

Reading

Reading is a good way to supplement your leadership skills. Learning from others' experience, good and bad, and learning the state-of-the-art tools are useful ways of expanding our repertoire of skills and knowledge. Widening the breadth of your reading material aids in developing your conceptual capacity. It is important to read all kinds of books, including books on subjects that may not particularly interest you. For instance, try reading fiction as well as nonfiction. If you love biographies, try science fiction. If you love historical novels, try mysteries. Reading outside your comfort zone allows learning to occur. You begin to find patterns in the different genres, to discover connections you hadn't noticed before. Reading on a broad range of topics is a great way to stimulate learning.

Experience

Experience on the job is a common way that executives learn. If you want to expand this learning significantly, take a position outside your normal line of work or career trajectory. Doing so will greatly enhance your learning opportunities. As with reading, it will cause you to learn a new culture, as well as new ways of operating, frames of reference, and rationale.

For instance, if you are a military officer, a two-year assignment working for a Congressional committee would be a great learning opportunity. If you work for the government, taking an assignment as a liaison with a trade organization would undoubtedly provide you with new and useful insights. If you are in the private sector, try making a lateral move that will give you a completely new perspective.

Experiences such as these force you to learn parallel perspectives and operating styles.

Take a look at the leaders of our nation. You will see that most of them didn't have a straight path career trajectory. Instead, they moved from one line of work to another, from the executive branch to the private sector, from handling legal issues to foreign policy to defense to domestic concerns. There is no uniform path. Most successful leaders have a wide range of experiences to draw from because of this variety, and these experiences have helped to "densify" their conceptual framework and expand their repertoire of skills. Experience, reading, and training are important ways to prepare for the executive level, but reflection is the day-in and day-out way that executive leaders learn.

Coaching

Coaching is another commonly used method for executive learning. Executive coaching comes in a variety of forms and is ultimately tailored to the needs of the client. A coach can be a thought partner or someone who serves as a sounding board. A coach can help the executive see how he is currently dealing with an issue, as well as alternative ways of dealing with the same issue. The coach can help the executive understand the environment and be comfortable with the uncertainty, unpredictability, and volatility of that environment. A coach can help the executive diagnose problems with teams or misalignments of systems, which is very important as either of these could be causing missed targets or failure to meet expectations. A coach can be a trusted partner who helps the executive understand and apply new tools of leadership. Executive coaching, conducted one-on-one where confidentiality is assured, can reduce the feeling of loneliness at the top and can help the executive navigate treacherous waters. A coach can help an executive learn and grow personally in a completely confidential setting. Executive coaching is customized "just-in-time" learning for leaders of an organization or company. Coaching as a sector of management services continues to grow as executives understand the tremendous return on investment possible from learning from certified and experienced executive coaches. Coaching works well at the executive level, but will produce measurable results at lower levels as well.

Resiliency

Resiliency is the result or by-product of learning. It allows you to get back up and lead when you have been knocked down. When you receive "360 degree" feedback that is less than stellar (and we all have), resiliency is your ability to get back on the horse that threw you. Everyone gets knocked down, suffers setbacks, and is disappointed as an executive. I don't know anyone who hasn't felt beat up by the system, people in the system, or the people around them at one time or another. You are not alone!

This knock down, failure, or misstep can come in many forms, e.g., a poor performance evaluation, a health setback, an ethical lapse, being fired, or being transferred out of your leadership position. Most executives don't talk about these episodes because it's risky: it can hurt your brand, your promotion potential, or your employability. For those executives or leaders who are in the public eye and face a blow of one kind or another, setbacks can be particularly devastating. Some never recover.

When a misstep happens, good leaders tend to rely on their self-confidence; the very same self-confidence that got them into the leadership position in the first place. They roll up their sleeves, have an honest conversation with themselves, and then recreate themselves. They not only bounce back, they bounce forward. And it's not that they sweep their failures or missteps under the carpet, but they have an ability to learn from mistakes and weather the risks of leadership better than most.

It is interesting to watch national public figures face tremendous scrutiny and have the capacity to bounce forward. Remember Hillary Clinton as our First Lady. She was criticized for her role in advocating public health policy. Detractors were brutal. She was subpoenaed to testify about the Whitewater controversy. She was criticized by feminists for standing by her husband during the Lewinsky scandal. Weathering these storms, she has proven to be nothing if not intelligent, confident, and resilient. She ran for office, served as Senator of New York, was narrowly defeated by Barack Obama for the Democratic Presidential nomination, and ultimately served as an exemplary Secretary of State.

General David Petraeus, a highly decorated military commander and politically appointed Director of the Central Intelligence Agency. With his keen political skills, he was considered to be a brilliant strategist and a potential candidate for our nation's highest office. Yet all of the trust and confidence he had spent a lifetime building was lost in a moment in 2012 when an extramarital affair surfaced. He promptly resigned from public office and public life. Despite such an ethical lapse exposed publicly, General Petraeus recognized his personal failings and bounced back. He has begun to speak publicly again and has accepted various positions which put him back in the public eye.

These leaders learned from their past mistakes and recovered their loss of trust. They retained what was good, strong, and positive about themselves. They forgave themselves, but most importantly, they learned. And with new lessons, insights, and knowledge from their experiences, they moved forward and put themselves back into the leadership arena. Personal resiliency is another way of learning about failures and surviving them to become a better leader.

In addition to personal resiliency, institutional resiliency is an important focus for an executive. As an executive, you have the latitude to strengthen your systems, including your systems of learning, staff development, and/or investments in the future leadership of your company or organization. For example, the arena of change management is worth investing in, in my opinion. The failure rate for leading change is high. It is complex and riddled with emotional and human behavior challenges. It takes a fair degree of skill to lead change at the enterprise level, or at any level, for that matter. In the increasingly volatile and complex world in which we operate, our ability to change and change fast makes a difference in our national security and our economy, and the demand for these skills will only increase.

Growing Importance of Change Management Skills

Change management leadership is so important that some private-sector leaders are contemplating establishing a requirement for a "change management" certification as a prerequisite to leadership positions. Other companies have nested a change management unit inside their company as a resource for their leaders and teams. In my view, those who do this are cutting-edge companies. As executives, it behooves us all to invest in learning more about the process of change management and to develop the skills in emerging leaders that will allow them to effectively facilitate change.

Contingency

We've all seen institutions that constantly operate in crises mode. No sooner does one crisis end than the next begins. Staff members are stretched and stressed as a result of constantly managing crises. They do the best they can with the time they have, but they are performing sub-optimally, as is the company or organization. The reasons for such crises are perhaps many; however, it is likely that the lack of time to stop, think, and methodically take action to bring the institution into balance and move forward toward the vision and goal is a significant factor.

As finely tuned as your business intelligence from external stakeholders may be, as sharp as your industry analytics are, as thorough as your strategy and tactics are, you will still face unforeseen circumstances. Without a doubt, you will have to deal with a surprise event that disrupts your business plans, throws off your strategy, and creates chaos, at least temporarily. It happens despite the best predictors, warning systems, and mitigation measures. As an executive, you must be prepared for unforeseen events.

While you don't have a crystal ball in which you can see the future, it is your job to hold 5% of your time in reserve so that you can respond thoughtfully to unpredictable events. If you have the time reserved, you will be better positioned to respond without disrupting the entire organization with less than carefully considered actions. It is your responsibility to set aside time for contingency. Then, when you need it, the time is there. When you don't need it, you can invest your time in other aspects of your job.

Summary

Your job as an executive is to reflect, think, and learn every day, to continue to grow and develop as a leader. In addition to reflection, learn through other means like reading books across various genres, taking positions outside your area of expertise or industry, and/or hiring an executive coach. Resiliency after a setback is the by-product of learning and a result of reflection. While no one can predict the future or foretell unforeseen events that significantly disrupt the organization or company, you can prepare for these eventual occurrences by reserving 5% of your time in the event of a crisis or unimaginable disruption.

Chapter Eleven concludes the discussion of the elements of the executive leader's job and the relative amounts of time that should be spent on each. Executive leadership is not easy. In Part II of *Sharing Secrets*, I'll ensure that aspiring leaders and those with executive leadership in their future are ready to lead. They will be set with lessons from other leaders and prepared to become great executive leaders.

Chapter Eleven Secrets

1. Develop your personal "feedback mechanism." Use your daily reflection time to review what went well and why and what could have gone better and how. Commit to adjustmentments to improve your leadership skills.

2. Know how you learn best and seek opportunities to learn through that means, manner, or method.

3. Commit to being a lifelong learner. Become or remain curious.

4. Read across a variety of genres, even those that aren't appealing to you.

5. Take on challenging assignments that may be out of your normal line of work.

6. Engage an executive coach to help you solve workplace problems with concrete skill development.

7. When you suffer setbacks, learn from them and reassert yourself as a leader.

8. Allow time for contingencies.

Chapter Eleven Exercise

Drawing on feedback from peers, supervisors, or subordinates, identify one skill or behavior you would like to improve. Create a six-month development plan that includes the following elements at a minimum:

1. Read: *FYI: For Your Improvement*[42] is a good starting point.

2. Train: Identify an online course or webinar.

3. Observe: Watch a mentor or someone who exhibits your desired skill expertly.

4. Attempt: Try out the new skill and seek feedback.

{ PART II }

Chapter Twelve

{ # ARE YOU READY TO LEAD? }

Warning! Be careful what you wish for. Executive leadership is not easy. For the good of the organization or company, for your department and team, and for you, it is important that you are ready to lead at the executive level before you start. The question then becomes, how do you know whether you are prepared? How can you be sure that you have had the necessary training and experience and developed the intellectual and emotional capacity to be an executive leader?

In Part I, I laid out the job of the executive. Reading it, you now know what the job is and what it is not. You know where to focus your time and why. You know the secrets for being a great leader, and you understand the many counterintuitive aspects of executive leadership. You are now ready for the role of executive leader. But wait!

There is one more overriding key to success at the executive level, which will be evident in the very best leaders: They are authentic. This means that they know themselves well and they are themselves all the time. They are comfortable with being vulnerable. These two aspects generate the level of trust that is needed for transformational change and truly great leadership.

Your staff, stakeholders, and bosses want to know that you have integrity. Honesty goes without saying. Even more, they want to know that you are well-meaning and that you have good intentions. They want to know that you have sufficient skills or the natural ability to do the job. In short, they want to know that they can trust you to know what you are doing. This relates back to knowing what your job is as an executive and what it is not. Beyond this, there is an intangible sense great leaders emit, and it comes from knowing themselves, being comfortable with themselves, and being vulnerable among their colleagues. Learn about yourself and you will find you have this trait, too.

Authenticity: Know Yourself, Be Yourself

To be a great leader is to know your fears, values, hopes, and dreams. As you rise to the role of executive leader, be willing to look at the source of your fears. Look back on major events of your life, both positive and traumatic, and examine what impact these have had on your life, the way you interact with people, your relationships, and the way you lead.

For example, I have experienced a number of traumatic events, and for the longest time I would not even talk about them. Remember the question, "Do you want to dance?" Well, in one case, saying "yes" led to the best decision in my life and for my career. My dance partner became my husband. But, years earlier, a "yes" to the same question led to a horribly traumatic rape. I didn't tell anyone about it for many, many years.

I have also seen death in a number of countries. I witnessed a murder in Haiti and, except for reporting it to the regional security officer, never talked to anyone about it. As a Peace Corps volunteer, I saw a lifeless body lying on the sidewalk and one hanging from a tree. Rather than talk about these traumatic events, I intentionally suppressed them.

In another instance, at the encouragement of my executive leader, I engaged in a risky border crossing to save the life of a subordinate, and then was instructed to eliminate the entire episode from my memory. Another time, during an official visit to South Africa, I ran as a colleague, Gary Hansen, was mugged at gunpoint. I didn't share these events with colleagues, much less write home about them.

These extremely frightening and traumatic events shook me to the core and had a profound impact on who I am. These were the most damaging secrets to keep, because they had such an impact. They changed me in ways I might not have been conscious of at the time.

For example, after the rape, I beat myself up. I replayed over and over the trauma and repeatedly asked, "How could I be so stupid? Why did I say 'yes' to a stranger? Why did I put my drink down and pick it up after the dance? Why did I step outside the club to talk to this stranger?" In short, I blamed myself. I repeatedly told myself I was dumb. Looking back years later, I could see where this was the beginning of a pattern where any little thing that went wrong, I attributed to a lack of smarts on my part. If I mispronounced a word, I was stupid. If I didn't get a joke, I was dumb—never mind that you 'had to be there' to understand it. If I made a wrong turn driving, I was stupid. After a while and without even being aware, this kind of self-talk took a toll on my self-esteem and self-doubt seeped in. My response was to gradually build walls. I intentionally did not let people get close to me. I worked extra hard to compensate for my self-perceived lack of smarts. I avoided talk of my personal life and engaged so fully in my professional life that work became all encompassing. There was a deep divide between my personal life and my professional life. I had fewer and fewer truly close friends. If things got hectic at work, I simply worked harder rather than ask for help. I simply didn't want anyone to get close enough to me to find out my secrets. As I began to climb the career ladder at work, I assumed it was all just good luck, certainly not attributable to any innate ability or effort on my part! Rather, I felt a like an imposter and was sure that someone was going to find out. I was so one-sided, I had a hard time engaging in nonwork conversations. I could talk for hours on any number of work topic, but I avoided any focus on me. The fear steered me toward work where I was safe. Under the normal stress of executive positions, I was pushed to my extremes—hyper-hardworking, hyper-strategic, hyper-critical, etc… These extremes and this imbalance prevented people from knowing me and prevented me from being vulnerable and authentic. The façade impacted my relationships and, as a consequence, my leadership. My ability to earn trust and to gain followers, despite ample skill in other areas of leadership, suffered. These secrets held me back until, in a moment of insight, I began to put the pieces together.

Now, I see how these events—and, more importantly, my insistence on keeping quiet about them—impacted my relationships and my leadership. I simply didn't know how an event like a rape or witnessing a murder could impact my life, behaviors, preferences, and reactions. I now know that I am not unique. Traumatic events and keeping them secret affect you, too!

Keeping secrets is understandable. It is a self-protective mechanism. We hold personal secrets because of fear. Some of us fear we are not smart enough or do not have enough social grace. Others of us fear the repercussions of exposure of some kind of humiliation like a rape, a criminal background, an arrest, or a drug or drinking problem. Others may have experienced domestic violence, bullying, or discrimination. Still others have been fired from their jobs, or failed in some very public way with a moral or ethical lapse. However, it is the secret itself and the fear of its exposure that hold us back from being our true selves and that ultimately hold us back from success.

In my case, I didn't seek help for a long time. I guarded each of these traumatic events and held them inside, in secret, out of shame, fear, and humiliation. It was the secrets more than the events themselves that had me in a stranglehold. After a lot of introspection and honest conversation with a therapist and my spouse, I began to see the adverse impact these events had had on my development and my relationships. This sort of personal introspection is what I am talking about when I say, "Get honest with yourself and know yourself well." Only when you know yourself can you be your authentic self. And only when you are your authentic self can you lead well.

In addition, the better you know yourself, the more internally aligned you are. And as you move toward greater internal alignment, you become happier. When you are aligned, you are at peace and when at peace you experience true joy. So, get honest with yourself. Share your secrets. Unlock the shackles of fear. Sharing your secrets with those close to you is the key. Examine their impact on you and your behavior patterns. Get ready to discover your true self. You will not regret it and you will be a better executive leader because of it.

Vulnerability

It seems counterintuitive, but leaders who share their vulnerabilities are actually stronger. When you know and are comfortable with yourself, it is much easier to be vulnerable. Most of us relate to people who are vulnerable. What does it mean to be vulnerable? It means knowing that you don't know it all and you are okay with other people knowing so. It means knowing your imperfections and celebrating your differences. People who are vulnerable have no problem saying, "I need help," "I don't know," or "I disagree. Help me understand your perspective." The formula goes like this: vulnerability is key to being authentic; being authentic is key to building trust; and building trust is key to gaining the followers you need to achieve your vision and goals. Looking at it from this perspective, it becomes clear that achieving your goals and vision begins with being and knowing yourself and aligning your personal values with the vision and goals of your company or organization.

Vulnerable people are easy to relate to because they evoke emotions and emotions are contagious. At first it may be a feeling of likeness or similarity, but it can lead to genuine love, which is the most powerful emotion in the human emotional lexicon. Love is the foundation of trust. It is the one commodity, resource, or power that is limitless. And, it is a powerful resource, because it can transform people. Love cannot be faked or pretended. It must be genuine. It must emanate from your soul. And you must know yourself and love yourself before you can love others. Love is the core of trust and, as you know, trust is essential to everything an executive leader is responsible for achieving.

These connections are secrets to success. When you are authentic and vulnerable, you know your job. You can be confident in everything you do. You don't have to know how to do everything; you don't have to have all the answers. On the contrary, you are confident that, among your team, the answers will emerge and together you will achieve your vision and goals.

Misaligned Promotion Systems

It is ironic that many promotion systems are misaligned in a way that actually discourages vulnerability, despite its importance. Vulnerability is an important aspect to nurture and develop in staff. By encouraging vulnerability, when people cross the threshold to executive leadership, they continue to exhibit it, which will help them build trust with their staff and, as a consequence, to achieve organization and company goals. Yet, the typical competitive promotion system discourages vulnerability. Because you are competing for the next promotion, you may carefully guard your brand or corridor reputation. You may be reluctant to reach out for help for fear that bosses will think you don't know what you are doing or subordinates will think you are in over your head. The competitive nature of the executive position discourages vulnerability.

On a larger scale, our competitive culture doesn't allow for letting down your guard, sharing secrets, admitting mistakes, learning openly from errors, but we sure do need it! Our institutions need it to become stronger and more effective. Our political system desperately needs it. As individuals, we need it. If we are to be more resilient and less hard on ourselves, we need to hold more realistic expectations of our leaders and ourselves. It is a myth that great leaders make no mistakes. All leaders inevitably make mistakes; that is how they grow into great leaders.

Executive Leadership Readiness Checklist

As far as I know, there isn't a checklist of attributes necessary for entry into the executive ranks. And it is no wonder, because leading at the executive level requires a lot of all positive attributes and skills and none of the negative ones. Therein lies a large part of the reason, perhaps, why such a large percentage of new executives fail. We expect too much of our executive leaders. All you can do is prepare yourself adequately and surround yourself with a support system to deal with the setbacks, which are inevitable and just part of the job. Every executive faces shortcomings, disappointments, and her share of mistakes. That is okay! That is how we learn.

Table 12.1 provides a checklist I've created of elements and experiences that will prepare you to distinguish yourself as a great executive leader.

	Table 12.1: Executive Leadership Readiness Checklist
1	Gather a breadth of experience. Experience in fields, companies, or organizations other than the one you are in. For instance, work in the legislative branch if you are in the executive branch, work in private sector if you are in the public sector, work a variety of technical issues, work in an academic institution and an advocacy organization. The more varied experiences you have, the better.
2	Live/travel abroad. Experience other cultures; live and work for some period of time in other countries and your depth of understanding will increase; learn/speak a foreign language(s) helps tremendously.
3	Read a breadth of materials. Stay abreast in your field of expertise through reading; keep up on what the thought leaders in leadership are researching and; read fiction of various genres.
4	Develop interpersonal maturity. Listen for, read, interpret, analyze, and tailor your emotions to the requirements at hand. This includes having a personal demeanor that invites trust through empathy and humility.
5	Develop critical thinking skills. It is important at both the strategic and tactical levels to develop a well-honed ability to analyze, evaluate, and synthesize system-wide issues. This includes thinking creatively as well as interpreting and relating external environment and global trends to your organization or company.
6	Embrace vulnerability. Understand the risk of being open to criticism and be willing to lead despite it. Understand the relationship between vulnerability, trust, developing people, and achievement of vision, goals, and strategy.
7	Manage conflict/operate successfully in teams. Conflict is inevitable. Viewing it as a positive opportunity to learn is the kind of perspective that you will need.
8	Love learning. No one is perfect and we all make mistakes; however, leaders' mistakes are on a stage for all to see. A good executive is at ease with the notion of scrutiny and employs a systematic process of continual learning.
9	Accept uncertainty. Develop the ability to operate without all of the answers and when knowledge is incomplete. Some people have a tendency to make a decision just to have certainty, but but this creates a false sense of certainty.
10	Be comfortable with volatility. Volatility, the rapid pace of change, and environmental turbulence are part of your job. Be cognizant, aware, and okay with the fact that speed and agility can make or break your organization or quickly render your company obsolete, and manage this volatility without undue stress.
11	Manage ambiguity. Be confident in your ability to manage ambiguity, to take initiative sometimes without clarity or direction; to lead when the meaning of an event or significant factor is not clear.
12	Be a visionary. Develop the ability to interpret the environment and project into the future. Develop the ability to "see around the corner" and predict future events based on decisions that have already been taken or events that have already occurred.
13	Reflect. Develop an appreciation and practice of regular reflection, not only for yourself, but as an example for others to emulate.

This Executive Leadership Readiness Checklist is not exhaustive, but it is representative of the skills, habits, and attitudes you will need to succeed at the executive level. Rate yourself on these 13 components to determine your readiness for the executive level. Don't be too hard on yourself; most current executives would not be able to check all 13 elements. Commit to continually learning and strengthening your abilities, processes that will serve you well in your career and in life.

Summary

Executive leadership is not easy. It behooves aspiring executives to know what their job consists of and what is outside the realm of executive leadership. Beyond knowing your job, it is equally important to know and be yourself. Authenticity and vulnerability are essential in developing the levels of trust and the kinds of positive emotions you need to support transformational change and institutional visions and goals. Whether you are an aspiring executive, a new executive, or a talent manager charged with recruiting executives, the Executive Leadership Readiness Checklist will help distinguish how prepared you are to lead at the executive level.

Chapter Twelve Secrets

1. Know your job: what it is, what it isn't, and how you should spend your time as an executive.

2. Know and be yourself. Be authentic.

3. Exhibit vulnerability. It develops trust and support for your leadership.

4. Develop the breadth and depth you need to excel at the executive level, as described in the Executive Leadership Readiness Checklist.

Chapter Twelve Exercise

Get honest with yourself. Think about the following statements and answer them honestly.

1. I am afraid of _____ because _____.

2. I avoid _____ because I worry that _____.

3. What experiences am I afraid to share?

4. Think and/or write about what you learned from these exercises.

Chapter Thirteen

{
# THE FLOOR OF EXECUTIVE PERFORMANCE
}

This chapter is intended to give you pause. It describes poor leadership styles. These are included so that you can, by contrast, consciously determine what kind of leader you want to be and not be. It is also designed to alert you to leader and/or subordinate behavior patterns that are likely indicative of poor leadership styles.

If you are fortunate, you have had at least one truly great leader in your chain of command or in your work environment who you want to emulate. With that leader in mind, you can easily identify attributes, characteristics, or behaviors that this leader routinely exhibited, like being fair, transparent, inclusive, open-minded, unshakeable, smart, strategic, compassionate, and ethical. These are the behaviors you'll want to adopt and retain in your own leadership positions. However, adopting these positive attributes isn't automatic. You have to practice them until they become second nature.

Over the years, I've surveyed people at all different levels of leadership, from executives, senior leaders, and emerging leaders to managers and high-potentials. I asked them, "What are the most common issues you face in the workplace?" The vast majority of responses centered on issues of leadership. You've heard the term "toxic leader," no doubt. I firmly believe that there is no such thing as a toxic leader. There are leaders who exhibit behaviors that have a poisonous effect on the work environment, but I don't think these leaders are intentionally poisoning the environment. Some are unaware of their behavior and its impact. They simply aren't collecting and analyzing behavioral data or cues from those around them. They don't link subordinates' behavior to their own. Typically, these leaders know something is not right, but they can't pinpoint the problem. Others may be aware of the problem, but don't understand the cause; nor do they appreciate how subordinates are coping with their leadership style.

Personally, I've had some truly great leaders and worked with dozens of other officers who were destined to be great leaders. I have had only two poor leaders over the course of my career. In both cases, these leaders were unaware that there was any problem with their leadership style. They were both good people, smart, and well-intentioned. They simply didn't know themselves particularly well. Since they were not self-aware, they couldn't detect any patterns in their own behaviors that might be affecting the work environment. Although they had strong analytical ability, they didn't analyze their subordinates' behavior and relate it back to their own.

In one overseas post, I was a senior leader working for an executive who exhibited behaviors that could be characterized as "toxic." As the Director of the Democracy and Governance Office, I was charged with achieving impossible targets and managing a $150 million portfolio with a dozen staff and a couple dozen contracts or grants. The executive was brilliant, with years of experience and loads of confidence. He had struggled in previous executive positions and had not learned much about leadership from these experiences. He cared deeply about making progress toward alleviating poverty and hitting annual targets. However, why he cared was never clear to me. While he had a fairly low level of self-awareness, he thought a lot of himself. He was very controlling. At one point in our working together, he told me to change the direction of the program as quickly as possible. I immediately initiated discussions and actions to do so. A few days later, I proudly reported to him how much progress we had made in beginning to turn around the program. He asked why I had undertaken those steps. How was he going to explain the change to members of Congress, he asked? Why would I do such a thing? Surprised, and with self-doubt seeping in, I took notes carefully detailing every word he said. "Stop the ship and turn it back around." I returned to my office a little stunned, thinking I had misunderstood him during our initial meeting. I moved to undo the actions and reverse the steps I had taken. A week later when I just about had the program and staff back to where we had been two weeks prior, I was again called to the executive's office. He asked for a report and I listed the steps I had taken. At that point, he looked at me completely confused and asked me why I hadn't changed the direction of the program. I pulled out my notebook and recounted our last two conversations and he denied them, seeming to have no memory of our earlier exchanges!

Frustration surfaces when there is a big gap between reality and expectations. Raising one's voice is an expression of that frustration. This executive must have been continually frustrated and disappointed, because he was a screamer. He yelled at almost every one of my peers for one reason or another. Some of them took it personally, which resulted in intense stress. Others compartmentalized his behavior and dealt with it by taking all measures possible to avoid the executive.

I learned how to deal with this type of outrageous behavior by watching how his deputy interacted with him. By stepping back, I could see that his behavior was completely unacceptable and that no one should have to tolerate it. Second, I learned that the executive had certain triggers that sent him into either an attack or a hypercritical mode. These were things that called into question, directly or by im-plication, his abilities (cognitive, leadership, and/or memory). I used a defensive, self-preservation tactic of heaping praise on him and never claiming credit or attributing success to anyone but him. I wasn't proud of my behavior. I did it to survive a leadership style that was completely dysfunctional. And that's how a leader's poor behavior can cause subordinates to behavior poorly as well. It becomes a cycle of negativity that is self-perpetuating.

Ultimately, this executive left his post. I understand he was asked to retire and left USAID almost immediately thereafter. Most people learn after a personal or professional crisis, by seeking help and doing a lot of soul searching and introspection. I hope for his sake, he learned. We all learn through experience and I trust he did too.

However, the remaining staff members were traumatized and defensive, and self-protective behaviors had become the norm. Luckily, USAID brought in an experienced executive with a reputation for taking care of his people. In superhero style, the new executive took the reins. He rebuilt damaged relationships, the mission, and the staff. He slowed work down, got everyone on the same page, and allowed time for healing wounds.

While that experience was traumatic, it ended on a good note. I was unfortunate enough to experience another poor leader in a second post. As director of a program with a much larger portfolio, closer to $500 million, I was responsible for managing the multidisciplinary crossing of sectors including education, health, agriculture, and forestry. Our leader, much like the executive in the previous example, was extremely smart and well-intentioned. She was extraordinarily creative and could generate a dozen good ideas in a given day. Her downfall was, in my opinion, that she didn't fully understand her job or the fact that developing people was her top priority. She was extremely impatient for results. Beyond that she wanted nearly impossible results now! She set the bar high and didn't allow her very capable and competent staff the space or time to accomplish results. She pushed us to manifest her ideas, which had not been thought through and were not socialized within the mission of USAID. At a weekly meeting in her office, I sat across the desk from her, like a teacher with a student. I wanted to report our progress and let her know how I planned to spend my time in the upcoming week. However, rather than listen to what we were doing, she interrupted and piled on four or five new ideas. It was all I could do to write them down. There was no time for asking for a fuller explanation or clarity of the idea or resources to apply to make the idea happen. She often told me what to do, when to do it, and how to do it, and then did it herself. For instance, once she told me to call a senior person in the host country government to initiate an action. Before I could walk down the hall 50 feet to my office, she had picked up the phone and made the call herself.

I don't know what incited her, but there were times when she shouted at subordinates in public and in front of peers. She was known for yelling and for engaging in tantrums that included throwing objects and humiliating staff in front of others. She had a reputation for being intimidating. She exhibited little self-control when things didn't go her way. As in my previous post, I tried to cope with her, and my behaviors were negative. I avoided her and boosted her ego. Nothing seemed to help.

At one point, I role-played an intervention with her to prepare myself for what I imagined would be a slaughtering. I was looking for just the right time and place to talk to her. In a car on the way to a meeting with the Vice Minister of the Interior, an opportunity arose. I spoke. I told her that she couldn't continue to treat people as she had and expect people to work so hard for her, only to have her attack them. She began to cry and said that was not her intention. When the car pulled up to the building, we both stepped out wiping our eyes. We walked into the meeting. Another senior embassy official had arrived prior to us and had begun to engage the Vice Minister.

I thought that my intervention and blunt message would have some impact on her, but unfortunately, it did not. I tried to get others in the mission, some who had suffered her tyranny much worse than I had, to join forces with me to have a family "intervention" of sorts, but to no avail.

Given my previous experience, I knew her behavior was unacceptable. Evidently, the reports of her leadership style got back to Washington and a team of senior people came down to conduct a management review. It wasn't long after that that she left the mission and, shortly thereafter, the agency. While I have not seen her since, I have heard from her. It appears that she, like all of us hopefully, learned a tremendous amount from that episode, as painful as it was.

Poor Leadership Behaviors in Leaders and Subordinates

Poor leadership behaviors encompass a group of behavior patterns that have a negative effect on the work environment. They obstruct change agendas and impede achievement of the institutional vision, goals, and objectives. The following pages detail types of poor leadership, behaviors as well as potential reasons or causes for them. Table 13.1 details typical subordinate responses to each of the types of poor leadership styles.

Table 13.1 is a reference tool intended to focus your attention on your behaviors and the behaviors of subordinates to ensure that you are aligned and exhibiting the behaviors of a great leader. The first column at the left indicates the type of poor leadership. The next column shows the corresponding characteristic behaviors of poor leadership. The third column outlines the corresponding needs that are likely causing the leader to exhibit these poor leadership behaviors. Finally, the fourth column lists the coping behaviors found in subordinates that correspond to each of the poor leadership styles. You should watch for these behaviors in subordinates as indicators of problems in your own leadership style. For example, if subordinates are exhibiting extreme deference to you as the leader, if they aren't critiquing your ideas at all, and if they are keeping a detailed record of every conversation you have with them, these are symptoms of a micromanagement leadership style.

Table 13.1: Poor Leader Types and Corresponding Subordinate Behavior			
Type of Poor Leader	Leader Behaviors	Underlying Need	Subordinate Behaviors
Micromanager	-Do everything themselves -Intimidating -Inflexible timelines -Solving subordinates' problems & making their decisions -Piling on tasks	-Trust -Control -Certainty	-Let executive believe subordinate's ideas were originally leader's ideas -Don't criticize them or their ideas even when invited to -Keep a record of the leader's instructions and decisions -Depending on severity, seek to depart
Angry Managers	-Extremely high standards -Don't articulate rationale to convey importance of timing -Hard to please -Little self-control	-Happiness -Dominance	-Show extreme deference -Find out what triggers their anger and avoid doing it -Revert decisions to the leader -Report often -Check in with leader before decision is made
Favorites Players	-Want approval of others -Not comfortable with diversity -Likes the familiar	-Consistency -Inclusion -Certainty	-Agreeing with boss, even when in doubt -Not generating new ideas -Include leader in meetings -Uncooperative teams -Gossip
Unethical Leaders	-Doesn't recognize himself as independent of executive position -Doesn't know the rules well enough -Rationalizes behavior	-Risk Taker -Flexibility in the application of rules	-Out of sight discussions of behavior -Attempts to bring attention to unethical behavior internally -Validate perception with others -Report externally to inspectors, overseers, or auditors
Egotistical Leaders	-Overconfident in own knowledge and skill -Strives for perfection -Competitive	-Authority -To be right -More time	-Deal with their #2; avoid the leader -Empathize with leader -Exhibit independence -Set narrow work boundaries
"My Way or the Highway" Leaders	-Believes he knows best -Generates lots of ideas -Impatient for results -Doesn't know the job -Underestimates or undervalues other's contributions	-Self-esteem -Their ideas implemented -To be right	-Keep leader out of decisions -Shower praise on the leader -Provide frequent status reports -Keep input to major decision to a minimum to limit liability

Micromanagers

Micromanagement is when the executive encroaches on the authority of subordinates. It is apparent when the executive moves past "what to do" and "when to do it" into the "how it should be done" space. When an executive provides "solutions" to problems that subordinates are fully capable of making, he is micromanaging. When he gives subordinates tasks and sub-tasks, and keeps not only his own to-do list, as well as his subordinates' lists, he is micromanaging. When he gives subordinates more tasks to do without fully understanding what they are already doing and without fully explaining how each task fits with the vision, goal, or strategy, or when he underestimates the time it takes to complete a task, he is micromanaging.

Micromanagement implies that the executive could do the job better or faster themselves. No one responds well to being micromanaged. It sucks the enthusiasm out of subordinates. It eliminates the possibility of them learning and prohibits their development, which, remember, is the key responsibility of the executive.

Leaders micromanage because of a number of possible factors. Some simply don't know their job well. They believe they should continue to do what they did before they got into the leadership position. Perhaps, they have not been properly trained or they are unable to apply their training. They may not understand that leadership at the executive level is a fundamentally different job than leadership at a lower level. In this best case, they simply don't know any better. This is common among first-time executive leaders.

Micromanagement can emanate from personality preference extremes. Just like an extreme extrovert talks incessantly and seems to be either unaware or unable to control himself, most micromanagers are only comfortable with complete control and certainty. They may keep a running list of actions that everyone should be doing as a way to mimic control. They may be completely unaware of this controlling tendency. All they know is that they feel better when they feel in control.

For them, being out of control creates stress, which impedes their clarity of thinking and judgment, including their self-awareness. So the micro-management continues.

Micromanagement behaviors can be sourced to the executives' discomfort with uncertainty, ambiguity, complexity, or rapid change. One of the qualities that distinguishes good executives from poor ones is their comfort level with the environment in which they are expected to operate. By definition, the environment is complex, rapidly changing, and often uncertain and ambiguous. The environment and the issues executives deal with do not fit neatly into a crystal clear box. Leaders who are comfortable in this kind of environment thrive and excel. Those who are not at ease with uncertainty try and control the environment, and often they, their organizations, and their subordinates suffer as a result.

The issues that executives deal with are complex and it is human tendency to want to solve them "now." However, sometimes there are no immediate answers, and sometimes there are many answers. Sometimes, decisions have to be made in what appears like an ad hoc manner. Sometimes by making a decision to solve the problem, you change the very nature of the problem. Executives who don't understand this and rush to decisions so that they can have closure and certainty probably don't fully understand the complexity of the problem. Because they are uncomfortable with the environment, they do what they can or what they know. Often this manifests itself as exerting control in the form of micromanagement.

Another variety of micromanagement is found in executives who believe that subordinates' work is a direct reflection of them. They believe that every document or presentation needs to be a work of perfection, like they would produce. They believe that what their subordinates produce is a direct reflection of their personal work. It is not. It cannot possibly be. Editing documents or perfecting decision memoranda is a disempowering behavior. It can stifle and discourage subordinates. It eats enormous amounts of time. If executives are regularly up until 11:00 p.m. editing documents or doing emails, it is an indicator that something needs to change. Something is likely wrong with the system that produces lower quality work.

Angry Managers

Using anger to manage subordinates is an issue for some executives. Anger and frustration stem from the difference between expectations and reality. If an executive expects a subordinate to lay out rigorous thinking and analysis of options in his report, but receives something that falls short of that, she is frustrated. If she expects a task to be completed and finds out it is not, she is angry. The anger emanates from the difference between the executive's expectations (whether conveyed to the subordinate clearly or implied) and reality. Maybe the timing was really important, but this fact wasn't stressed to those leading the task. They didn't fully understand the importance of the task, and so weighed its completion with other priorities they were charged with, and made the decision to finish something else first. The executive's frustration, in this case, is her own fault, as she did not explain the rationale behind the deadline.

Anger is also a way to increase the risk of subordinates' taking decisions or actions. Subordinates want to avoid being subjected to the executive's anger, so they report out often, they check-in before making decisions, and in many cases just put decisions in the lap of the executive rather than make a wrong one. This is their way of lowering the risk of decision making or eliminating it all together. As you can see, the toll one angry episode can take on staff is profound. For executives who recognize that they are prone to anger, change is possible. Understanding the source of the anger helps, as does self-awareness. However, above all else, it is important to learn how to control your emotions. Episodes of anger are a major trustbuster and should be avoided it at all costs.

In response to angry management, subordinates develop all sorts of coping mechanisms. Some withdraw. Others keep a detailed log of conversations, actions, and meetings with the leader. Some report to the executive too often and some heap praise on her in an attempt to get on her good side as a hedge against an anger outburst. While these tactics may work for subordinates, the leader needs to be very attuned to such behaviors, because they are reactive signs to angry management. As an executive, if you spot these behaviors in your subordinates, seek anonymous feedback about the possibility that you are unintentionally using anger as a management tool. An executive coach is an excellent source for these kinds of conversations.

Favorites Players

Another toxic behavior that can destroy trust and result in a few people doing all of the work is favoritism. Naturally, there are some people or groups of people who perform better than others, and the executive will relate better to some groups or individuals than to others. Some executives show favoritism to those groups of people or individuals who think like him, understand him, and perform for him. It is natural to align with people with whom we feel an affinity, to give them the favored jobs or the trusted assignments. However, this is a trap!

Favorites players create an environment that leads to hyperempowerment of some staff members and disempowerment of others. Rather than work to understand the issues, the executive may lean more heavily on those with whom he aligns. This can be disastrous. A trustbuster, it will spiral into destructive gossip and uncooperative teams. Equal and even treatment of all subordinates is important to successful leadership. Aiming to understand and relate to those subordinates who are not like you or who may not fully understand you or your decisions is critical to maintaining the group cohesion necessary to achieve a vision and carry out the strategy. Resist the temptation to favor individuals or groups.

Unethical Leaders

I feel compelled to dwell a bit on ethics and ethical behavior. It could be a result of the 24-hour news cycle with more time to fill, technology surfacing news instantaneously, laws that demand greater transparency, or all of the above. However, it seems that we learn about another leader who fails because of an ethical lapse practically every other day. Some recent examples that have made national news include:

Bernard "Bernie" Madoff ran one of the most successful investment firms on Wall Street. Thousands of wealthy people trusted him to manage their investments to the tune of billions of dollars. Madoff, a prominent philanthropist, served on numerous nonprofit boards, including several that entrusted their endowments to him. He served as the prestigious chairman of the NASDAQ. Then, in 2008, it was revealed that his business was running a Ponzi scheme. This was the largest financial fraud in U.S. history. Madoff was arrested, charged, and convicted on numerous federal felonies and will spend the rest of his life behind bars.

Eliot Spitzer, former New York State Attorney General, had a reputation for fighting organized crime, securities fraud, and white-collar crime. He had everything going for him as the newly elected governor of that state, but was forced to step down in 2008 when, just slightly more than a year into his term, his involvement as a regular client of an escort service was exposed. Since then, Spitzer has been resilient enough to appear in a number of television roles as a political commentator and talk show host. Time will tell if he can win back the public's trust and reenter politics.

General William Ward, a four-star U.S. Army general, served at our nation's newest combatant commands, Africa Command. In 2011, after three-and-a-half years in the prestigious position, he was investigated for misuse of taxpayers' money. He used funds improperly and was ordered to repay $82,000 to the government. He retired as a demoted three-star general.

I think you get the picture. One day, we are celebrating and toasting these leaders, the next day we find out that they aren't who we think they are at all. Maybe it is the heightened focus on brand management that causes leaders to spin a tale of perfection and hero-like mythology. When these leaders misstep they fall hard. The most resilient among them step back for a few months before beginning their apology tour, but it is highly likely that they will never fully regain the public's trust. They certainly cannot regain the same stature and esteem they had before that trust was broken.

Types of ethical failures are varied, but following is a short list of the most common failures seen in government. Though some of these seem relatively minor, all carry serious penalties:

- Bribery
- Conflicts of interest
- Credit card abuse
- Political activity
- Misuse of government resources, including staff
- Abuse of positional power
- Accepting gifts
- Time and attendance violations
- Violations of travel authorizations and vouchering

As you look at the list, it is strange to think about executives violating the most mundane and routine processes like time and attendance. It is hard to imagine how much one could gain from violating travel procedures or processes. It is even harder to imagine that one would risk his career and, more importantly, his credibility, to step over the line. Yet, leaders do and it isn't that uncommon.

The private sector isn't immune to unethical behavior. If you think about it, the risks are even higher there. The executive in the private sector is part of the brand of the company. If she steps over the red line, the lapse can negatively impact the value of the company through impacting investment and growth.

Why do leaders lose their way? On the one hand, it is easy to see how it could happen. On the other hand, given the frequency of unethical behavior among executives, you would think they would have a heightened sense of awareness and be on guard against possible ethical slips. The difficulty is that executives are just people. Many people are poorly prepared to deal with success and the benefits and perks of the executive job. The "perks" are designed to aid the executive in successfully meeting the extraordinary requirements of the position. For instance, there is an expense account for entertaining and relationship building; a car and driver for the many external events, meetings and representational functions; and an executive assistant to help with errands, routine actions, and the calendar. These "perks" can slip into a gray area very quickly. For instance, your executive assistant can cross the line to becoming your personal assistant who runs personal errands, buys personal gifts on your behalf, and keeps your personal calendar. Unless those specific functions are part of the job, then your requests have crossed the line.

Executives can easily get an inflated sense of their own importance. Coupled with the characteristic stresses of the job and the infamous "lonely at the top" feeling, some executives lose touch with reality. They abandon rules or think they are above them or that the rules don't apply to them. Once that happens, it is a downward spiral that will ultimately end in a personal crisis.

To prevent this, you have to be on guard. You have to set the highest ethical standard possible for yourself. You must walk the talk, setting an example for how you expect others to speak and behave not just in public, but more importantly, behind closed doors when you are with your inner circle. Perception matters too. How you speak and behave privately matters as much or more than how you behave publicly. Know your values and live by them.

Let's take me for example. I consider myself to be an ethical person. While Mission Director at USAID, I worked with my controller and executive officer to ensure that I followed all the rules governing "benefits," including the use of the car and driver, the use of the house, entertaining, and so on. I don't pretend to be an expert on the rules and

I had to rely on my staff to keep me in compliance. It turns out the rules, strictly interpreted, allowed for much more than I actually received. I turned away a few benefits, because I felt that taking them could be perceived as questionable. The controller and executive officer agreed with me. It was better to focus beyond the rules and think about the perception. So, I did. I complied with the rules, but perception trumped the rules that left me with a more restrictive set of "benefits."

I was totally surprised during my 360 reviews when input from staff was solicited. Two of 12 people ranked me below average on ethics. I had suggested that these two employees be given a chance to rate my performance, because while they were high performers, I knew something wasn't right between us. I was crushed by the feedback. I didn't understand that rating. I thought I had taken all the steps to set a good example of strong ethics. By working with my executive coach, I came to terms with their ratings. The two people who rated me lower on ethics were the same people whose trust I had not gained. The ethics rating was more a reflection of the absence of trust than anything else. So, as I continued in my position, I made every effort to make statements that would clarify my ethical standards and build trust.

My point in sharing this example is that, while you may perceive yourself a certain way, there will be people who see you completely differently! To know how you are coming across to others, you have to ask them. A good way to do this is to put in place some measure of feedback for you as a leader. Assign someone on your staff to be the "pit bull," the person who has your permission to look for perceptions of unethical behavior—however slight—and call them to your attention. This won't happen automatically; you have to give the job to someone. Other things you can do are to establish a confidential "hotline" or email box where questionable behavior can be reported. Give the "pit bull" the responsibility to review and examine complaints. Then let her work independently; don't interfere. Be open and transparent in addressing all issues, even the appearance or perception of an issue, because all of these can erode trust and impede progress.

Note that sometimes what appears as one issue may actually be a reflection of another. Ethics can be a minefield to maneuver, but my suggestion is to know yourself, vocalize ethical behavior, and provide staff an opportunity to periodically assess your behavior. Then learn from that feedback. Openly behave to correct perceptions, adjust, and move forward. If you don't have a system in place to capture this kind of information, you could be losing staff or eroding trust without ever knowing what is driving it.

Everyone has different ethical guides. What is right and wrong to you is different from what is right and wrong to someone else. Ethics are not only cultural, but personal. Ethics guide your decisions, and very importantly, what I believe is ethical may be very different from what you believe is ethical.

That's why it is important to know how others perceive you. An action you take may be perfectly legal, but may still be perceived as unethical. When it comes to ethics, perception rules. Ensure that all of your actions can withstand the "perception test" of ethics.

When you have established greater trust with your subordinates, they will cut you slack on decisions that may or could be interpreted as unethical or borderline unethical. When you do not have high levels of trust, they will find ethical issues in the most surprising places. The lesson here is to build and maintain high levels of trust, get input on your decisions, and raise questions about perceptions and ethics and listen to the feedback and input you receive.

Egotistical Leaders

We all know egotistical leaders. These are executives who seem to create crises where none exist. They seem to thrive on the adrenaline that comes from being involved in crisis situations. The crisis may be "self-inflicted," i.e., caused by a lack of planning or an inability to interpret trends, or it may result from the complexity of a problem. What to note here is that the egotistical leader enjoys swinging into action, tasking and subtasking, orchestrating the timing, and pulling off the nearly impossible. He enjoys swooping in like a superhero and when the nearly impossible is achieved, he claims victory, reveling in the accolades and praises thrown his way.

A similar case is when nearly impossible performance targets for a change agenda are established and pursued with vigor. The targets are linked to the executive's performance calendar. If annual evaluations are in March, then in February subordinates see an uptick in interest from the executive in achieving annual targets. If bonuses are provided in October, then the weeks before bonus decisions are made the executive drives staff extremely hard. Then there is the double whammy: the executive's presentation of the change agenda and the rationale for the change are directly linked and timed to help fulfill his desire for promotion, bonuses, or fame. This is occasionally apparent among politically appointed leaders in government who view their leadership positions as a stepping stone to greater, more visible positions (elected office or otherwise).

When the business case for change is your ego, you have a problem. This is a major trustbuster. Staff members figure this out very quickly and you lose your credibility. They may begin to go to your deputy to avoid dealing with you. They narrow their work boundries and exhibit extreme independence. Remember, your executive leadership position is not about you; it is about your staff and your company or organization. When you put your interests above theirs, you lose the very credibility and trust that you need to achieve the goals and strategy with which you are charged. So it may be counterintuitive, but the focus and drive should be on subordinates, their agendas, their timelines, and their motivators, not yours.

"My Way or the Highway" Leaders

Another category of poor leadership behaviors emanates from those bosses who are so inflexible that they honestly believe their way is the best and only way. They are directive to the point of being authoritarian. They love and exploit the hierarchical structures of the organization they lead. They are perceived as a royal tyrant. Possibly without even knowing it, they are very status-conscious. They perceive questions or counterarguments as direct threats to their status as the boss. When their status is threatened, it creates stress.

If you have this tendency as a leader, subordinates may try to keep you out of decisions for fear that you will take over. Some may try and engage you and discuss how leaders in the same or similar positions acted previously. Others may stroke your ego by making comments about your brilliance. In a work environment like this, the questions and counterarguments disappear, and staff will let the leader make less-than-optimal decisions as a way to reduce their liability and push the full responsibility for the decision onto the leader. As a leader, if you see these signs, stop and seek feedback. Seek help from an executive coach to improve your leadership style. Remember that your job is to make only those decisions that others can't.

Summary

One of the ways to know if you are ready to be an executive or to become a great executive is to fully develop your self-awareness, self-control, and self-management. Use your reflection time to assess how certain situations make you feel. Replay conversations or meeting dynamics to reexamine your initial assumptions. Could it be that other assumptions are equally valid? This kind of reframing will aid you in making more accurate interpretations of intentions. Reflection is the time to develop actions that will allow you to have better conversations, facilitate better meetings, and react more productively to emotional cues. And, like with anything else, you get better with practice.

If you want to avoid any of the destructive leadership styles and behaviors discussed in this chapter, the best thing you can do is to find someone you trust to be honest with you and to listen to you. During my appointment in Peru, I had one person who did this for me. Bill Gelman would come into my office, shut the door, sit down, and give me feedback about decisions I might be making, a communication I had had, or how I was spending my time. I didn't always agree with him, but I appreciated the feedback. Once I learned the value of having someone who would give me such straightforward feedback, I looked to establish that person in every subsequent position. This person isn't necessarily your deputy or number two. It could be the head of human resources, who is trained to detect and deal with these kinds of issues. It could be an external or internal coach. It could be a friend who has known you for a long time and who cares about your well-being. It matters less who it is than that you give someone the job of being honest with you and that you listen to him or her.

In Chapter Fourteen, we will examine how important leadership is to team dynamics and to building high-performing teams.

Chapter Thirteen Secrets

1. Understand your job as executive and resist encroaching on others' authority.

2. Learn to read subordinates' behavior patterns as an indicator of executive leadership style.

3. Avoid directing "how" to complete a task, an assignment, or responsibility.

4. Understand your source of frustration or anger and manage your emotions.

5. Treat all subordinates equally. Don't walk into a favoritism trap.

6. All your actions should withstand the "perception test" of ethics.

7. Assign a "pit bull" and give her the authority to bring issues to your attention.

Chapter Thirteen Exercise

Take a look at yourself. Do you currently see any of these poisonous behaviors in your leadership style? Solicit feedback from trusted peers and honest subordinates. Ask what skill or strength they would like you to exhibit more. Which behaviors would they like to see less? Examine their feedback with a keen eye toward the weaknesses outlined in this chapter. Then, make a developmental plan to address these areas.

Chapter Fourteen

{ GO TEAM GO! }

Much of what we accomplish on the job is done as a member of a team or by teams that we lead. Thus, the functioning and performance of teams, particularly senior or executive teams, is an important focus of the executive leader.

Why do we create teams? Because teams comprised of individuals with diverse perspectives, experiences, and strengths are smarter and stronger than any one individual. In creating a team, we bring together a group of people to work on problems, projects, and challenges.

In order for a team to perform optimally, achieve high-level tasks, solve complex problems, and operate in sometimes uncertain environments, the input and contributions of all members are needed. Without everyone's contribution, the product or result will not be the best it can be. It's like a favorite recipe: if you are missing one ingredient, at best the dish doesn't taste the same, and at worst it is inedible.

We learn about being a team member as youngsters. In the classroom and on the athletic field, we learn about team spirit and subordinating individual goals to the larger goal of the team. We learn to follow established rules. We learn discipline and hard work to support our team members. We learn how to use the strengths of every member of the team to achieve our goals, and we learn to follow the lead of the coach or teacher.

Some families have family goals and are great environments in which to learn teamwork. In my family, I was one of thirteen children. My father was a university professor and researcher and my mother supported us from the home. In order to achieve the family goal of sending all of us to the universities of our choice, my parents set up a college fund. From the time we could work, each of us contributed to the fund from our summer job earnings. My father contributed his summer teaching salary. Some of us had better-paying jobs in construction or roadwork. Others of us made minimum wage working at the local hamburger joint. But everyone contributed. When payday came, we simply endorsed our checks for deposit into the college fund account. The pooled resources were invested to earn more money, and, ultimately, depleted little by little over a period of 20 years to pay for all of our college educations. It was quite a team accomplishment! Some of us contributed more than our tuition and college cost and others contributed less. It didn't matter. We were all proud to be part of such an ingenious system and working toward such a significant goal.

The challenge about teamwork is this: Even if you have positive experiences from childhood, it can be rather unnatural to work as a team. It seems more "normal" to work as individuals. Often no one explains to the team members what the team dynamics should be or even what to expect as a member of the team. For instance, if you've led in one team environment, should you assume a leadership position in another? Team members tend to fall back on their strengths and contribute where they can without much direction regarding why they are on the team, what is expected of them as team members, and what the boundaries are. They assume that, above all else, they should represent their home unit or organization and not cede ground, as if in a competitive environment. In practice, that is exactly what you don't want.

Forming the Team: Cohesion and Vulnerability

The first thing a team should do is to cut loyalties to the home unit. Jerry Hyman, one of my earlier and best supervisors and now a senior advisor and president of the Hills Program on Governance at the Center for Strategic and International Studies (CSIS), used to say, "Where you stand depends on where you sit." It is so true! Team members, especially cross-company units or interagency teams, come to their new team with the loyalty and pride of their old team or their home team. They question whether this new team has priority over the old team. Will they ultimately be accountable to the home team, agency, or unit? How will their actions be received or viewed by the home team? Should they represent the interests of the home team?

Traditional stovepiping is inevitable given the size of many companies or the government, but it can impede progress, especially transformational progress. Stovepiping often hampers team performance because it is tough for people to shift allegiances. Sometimes they simply don't see the bigger picture. Sometimes they can't see the limits of their narrow focus or specialization. Sometimes they cannot see the benefits, the value added that they could gain from joining forces with others, especially if the other has a different view on issues or a distinct agenda.

The aim in the initial steps of forming a group is to increase cohesion, or how well the members of the group support each other in working together. Cohesion comes from trust and vulnerability. If there has been a history of interactions between members of the group, this history must, at a very minimum, be acknowledged before group cohesion can be achieved. If there has been discontent among team members in the past, then it must also be addressed before moving ahead. In some cases, mediation or time-out sessions to probe the source of discontent and distrust are needed before the team can move forward. It is your job to coach or engage a coach to deal with the history or mistrust that is impeding group cohesion.

Group cohesion provides an atmosphere that allows members to take risks without fear of being ridiculed or criticized harshly. Individuals feel more comfortable putting forth their positions, rationale, and out-of-the-box ideas, as well as having others ask questions about their ideas without feeling attacked. Group cohesion allows you to build off of others' ideas and build up their arguments by looking critically at them. It increases learning, idea generation, and innovative solutions, all of which can lead to higher productivity, increased efficiency, and larger profits for companies or improved effectiveness for organizations.

Vulnerability is the secret ingredient to the kind of team spirit that distinguishes between good and great performances. If you can create an environment where asking for help or saying "I don't know" is viewed neutrally rather than as good or bad, then you will be rewarded with a team spirit that will carry you to new heights. If you create an environment where arguing and discussion lead to improved products, then you have a highly functional team. Vulnerability, and the trust that it will not be violated, allow team members to be themselves, let down their guard, and feel accepted and valued. If you look at teams that exceed expectations and attain a high level of achievement, they have a spirit that is the product of vulnerability, trust, and knowing and appreciating each other's strengths.

It shouldn't make headline news but it does. In the *McKinsey Quarterly*, an article by Adam Grant showed the importance of supporting your peers and having your peers support you to good effectiveness.[43] If you've ever played on a championship athletic team, basketball for instance, you will recognize this as teamwork plain and simple. Even if you aren't on the team but are a follower, you can see how the five players on the court, the players on the bench, and the coach work together to achieve victory. They know each other's strengths and weaknesses, tee up their strengths, and call for help and step in where needed to minimize weaknesses. It is this selflessness that creates camaraderie and trust. In team athletics, there is no hiding a poor team member. You are on the court or field for all to see. If you screw up, your shot is blocked, the ball is stolen, you miss a pass, throw an "air ball," or even trip, you can't cover it up. You are fully transparent and vulnerable. Your teammates, more than anyone, know this. Teammates have a level of intimacy that is seen in few other places. It is this vulnerability and trust based in intimacy that allows teams to excel. It is this elusive team spirit that executives aim to create, because they know the power that this kind of sharing, giving, and taking can have on performance. Whether it is an athletic team, a team working on a new product, or a team solving complex problems, the hallmark of high performance is one where the team spirit is alive and well.

Aligning Incentive Structures with Team Performance

The operating principle common to all great teams is recognition. Credit for success is not given to just one member of the team. Instead, whether coming from the team itself, the executive, or others, credit is given to the team as a unit. When there is deviation from this principle, issues arise. In general during team operations, individual weaknesses are not spoken of. They are not ignored; they simply are not the focus. Instead, emphasis is on strengths and building on these. It isn't that teamwork is a love fest, but members recognize it simply isn't as productive to focus on weaknesses.

Reward systems often work against the promotion of teams. They are out of alignment with the vision and strategy in that they don't adequately reward teamwork and they value and reward individual performance. (Review Chapter Four for the discussion about alignment.) Typically, reward systems are competitive and focus on the individual. The higher you go in the organization, the more this is true. The annual appraisal attempts to capture the value you added to the achievement of yearly results. Annual evaluations often exaggerate individual contributions and minimize team contributions. You want your evaluation to be as strong as possible because you want to increase your chances of promotion with its attendant higher salary and greater responsibility.

This system doesn't capture the team aspects. You may have played a minor role in leading an achievement. Maybe you built off of others' ideas without giving them credit, thinking that giving others credit would somehow minimize your contribution. This is wrong! Another counterintuitive concept, credit for success is not a limited commodity, as mentioned earlier. You can give it away and still have plenty remaining. In spectator team sports, you can easily observe the relative contribution of each player. In the workplace and in annual evaluations, it is harder to measure.

Evaluation and reward systems work against the notion of vulnerability and trust. If you have to be vulnerable in order to gain trust and you have to have both in order to achieve great things, then the reward system should reward vulnerability and not its lack. Can you imagine the leader of your organization or company saying, "I don't know," or "I need help?" You probably can't. You expect him to know and be confident in his leadership, and he, in turn, is afraid not to meet that expectation. Similarly, if you are competing against several other people for a promotion, you are not likely to make yourself vulnerable in a team environment. The risk is that peers or superiors would conclude that you don't know what you are doing or that you are in over your head. It would work directly against a competitive promotion system that recognizes and rewards individuals. This disconnect in reward systems between team and individual leads to team members who are hesitant to be vulnerable, especially in a team environment.

However, you need to be vulnerable and to reward vulnerability if you are to become a great or even a successful organization or company. Vulnerability is the first step to building trust, group cohesion, and outstanding results or products. This is an issue of misalignment of systems and it is your responsibility, as the executive, to bring it into alignment with the vision, goals, and strategy.

A Group Is Not a Team

Not all groups are teams. Jon Katzenbach and Douglas Smith, both former senior executives at McKinsey and Company, point out the differences between groups and teams in their article, "The Discipline of Teams."[44] They point to working groups with strong leaders and individual accountability and compare them to teams with shared leadership, mutual accountability. The work products of working groups are individual; each individual in the group is responsible for a product within the group. Work products of teams are collective; everyone owns them and is responsible for their success. Within the working group, the team spirit that is generated from working together as a team is not apparent. As a result, I would argue that the levels of trust within and among team members are much higher than among members of a working group.

In my career, we had lots of working groups that we called teams, but which really weren't. The most prominent of these were the "country teams" at each embassy. These teams were comprised of the highest-ranking leader (the executive) from each department (Justice, Commerce, Defense), or agency (USAID, Federal Aviation Administration, Peace Corps) along with key Department of State executives, including the political officer, the deputy chief of mission, and the economic officer. Country teams typically met weekly for an hour-long meeting chaired by the embassy ambassador, but they didn't operate like a team or even like a working group. Rather, these meetings delivered updates to the ambassador and rarely accomplished anything beyond tasking an individual or department. One could say that the work product was the running of the embassy and achieving benchmarks and targets. However, the "country team" was not, in most cases, a team at all. That is not to say there weren't interagency working groups operating within an embassy, as there were. But the country teams were rarely "teams" by the terms or characteristics laid out in the literature.

Clarity Is Your Job

Don't short shrift your team by failing to set clear parameters or letting them become a real team. Selecting team members and laying out parameters are important parts of your job. CEOs can be too hands-off and simply assume that team members will figure out for themselves what the parameters are and what their roles should be. It's true, people are resourceful and can work together to figure this out, but why risk it? Better to be clear about the objective and precise in the parameters. Likewise, if your team is not functioning well, it is your job to lead it back to successful functioning or to disband it. People want to work in a well-functioning team. If it isn't functioning well, they may shy away from teamwork in the future.

Teams need clear expectations. Yet, more often than not, people are thrown together without direction. Teams need standards for operations, form, roles, objectives, duration, resources, and communication. The executive should present these when she establishes the team or clearly state what she expects the team to develop. Likewise, the exit plan needs to be clear from the start. The executive should articulate the duration or life of the team. Is the team established for a task or a function? Will it be a permanent part of the organization or will it exist through a certain period of the strategy? Will it be dissolved when the product or report is produced? Time and again, I have seen teams established without clear authority, task, duration, or resources. This creates confusion and can distract from group cohesion, which is so critical to team success and achievement.

In strong, well-functioning teams, members are self-policing. Since they all are responsible for the end product or outcome, members develop ways to hold each other accountable without focusing on weaknesses. Usually, peer pressure ensures that all members do their part, bring their best, and try their hardest to achieve success. It is recognized that everyone isn't at their best every day, and it is in knowing the strengths of team members and when and how to capitalize on them that makes a team function well.

Team Vocabulary

Words matter! Watch out for blocking words. They impede good teamwork. Put these words and phrases into the "unacceptable" category. At the top of the list is, "yes, but." The word "but" negates anything that comes before it, so when you say "yes," followed by "but," you aren't really saying "yes." Eliminate "yes, but" from team vocabulary.

Similarly, responding to teammates' ideas with, "We've tried that before and it didn't work," "that will never work," or "that will never work here," shuts down their contribution. Eliminate these as well. Judging words (especially when said in a condescending tone) like, "Really?" or "Be serious!" or "You've got to be kidding!" will evoke a similar reaction.

And it isn't just the words. Facial expressions and body language speak volumes. Imagine sharing your idea and watching your teammate respond with a patronizing smirk, raised eyebrows, or a sneer verging on laughter. All of these are just as harmful as words and cause people to shut down. These subtle and not-so-subtle communication patterns wreak havoc on team dynamics, cohesion, and, ultimately, productivity. As an executive, unless you are working with an experienced team that has demonstrated positive team behaviors, do not assume anyone will refrain from exhibiting destructive words and gestures. Make it clear from the outset that these are unacceptable because they are counterproductive.

Good team members are good listeners. The best ones are not only able to turn off a tendency to criticize, but they are also able to overcome their personal biases. If you've ever tried to do this, you know it isn't easy. It is practice and skill that makes a good team member. Great team members ooze respect and acknowledge others' ideas and points with ease. Their words and behaviors match. They are genuine. They ask for clarity when they don't understand rather than sit with a questioning look on their faces. They don't interrupt people when a new thought or idea pops into their head. They reflect, summarize, and even synthesize information and discussions.

And as this is true for teammates, so it is true for leaders. More than half of the people with whom you work will follow your lead based on the quality of your teammate-to-teammate interaction. Teams are a wonderful environment in which to learn and practice leadership qualities and skills.

Size Matters

As you are composing your team and placing people with varied skills, perspectives, experiences, and attitudes on it, ask yourself "How big is too big?" While there is no magic number, teams can become too large and unwieldy to manage. They lose their intimacy and cohesion. So make your teams only as big as they absolutely need to be.

Derailing Indicators

How do you know if your team is not performing, or worse yet, if it is dysfunctional? It is easiest to simply ask. In the absence of direct communication with the team, you will naturally look to quantitative performance indicators to tell you if the team is derailing or performing. In addition to performance indicators, here are some telltale signs that something has gone awry. You can observe these simply by attending a team meeting:

- One person takes over the team in a coup d'état style.

- Members don't show up for meetings; they don't feel they will miss anything.

- Decisions are made by one or two members rather than by the group as a whole.

- The motives of some team members are questioned by others; they appear to have their own, separate agenda.

- After the meeting, some team members gather in one member's office or common space to discuss the meeting.

- In the meeting, words and behaviors don't match.

If these or similar things are happening around your team, you will want to reiterate the objectives and parameters, including team behavioral norms. Any issues of broken trust will need to be addressed as part of your effort to get the team back on track. If these issues cannot be addressed and resolved amicably, then you may have to change the composition of your team. Of course, you hope it won't get to this point, but it does happen. Do your best to prevent the damage a derailed team can do by setting up the team for success from the beginning. Set parameters initially and check in periodically to determine if the team is on track.

Setting Parameters for High-Performing Team Success

If you aren't clear where parameter setting starts and stops, let me offer you this list of questions. The Executive Leader's Checklist for High-Performing Teams provides a list of questions that help establish the parameters for the team and sets them up for success. I highly recommend that you make sure the parameters listed in Table 14.1 are clear to all team members.

Table 14.1: The Executive Leader's Checklist for High-Performing Teams

☐	Who are the members of the team and what are their respective roles?
☐	Are there high levels of trust among teammates?
☐	What is the objective of the team's work and is it clear to each member?
☐	Does each member support the achievement of the objective?
☐	Is the objective viewed as critically important?
☐	Does each person know why he or she is on the team?
☐	What does each person bring to the team?
☐	Is the delegated authority clear?
☐	Does each member understand where the team assignment ranks among all other responsibilities he or she may have?
☐	Is a realistic timeline set and is that timeline understood by all?
☐	Does the team know what resources are at its disposal to achieve its objective?
☐	Have existing reporting lines been altered? If so, is it clear to all how and for how long?
☐	Who does the team turn to if it has issues or questions?
☐	What operating behaviors are acceptable and unacceptable?
☐	How will decisions be made by the team?
☐	Does each team member understand the difference between meeting and exceeding expectations?
☐	If the objective is not met, what happens? What is at stake?

Ensuring that all team members understand the parameters of the team is the best way to ensure that high-performing teams achieve success. Done correctly, the team dynamics that result from this investment will yield a whole greater than the sum of its parts. It will also contribute to staff development (the executive's number one priority) as team members will experience success in their work together. Once the teamwork is complete, chair a session to cull lessons from the team process and to formally conclude the work of the team.

Summary

Much of what is accomplished is done by teams and because of that the functioning and performance of teams holds particular importance for an executive. Especially for senior teams, forming the composition of the team and establishing group cohesion is the focus of the executive. Establishing clear parameters for the team heightens their chance of success as does aligning incentive structures. Don't assume that because you are dealing with adults, they know how to perform on a team. When establishing your team, use the Executive Leader's Checklist for High-Performing Teams (Table 14.1) and make sure everyone has clarity about the parameters for the team. If need be, provide the parameters in writing to avoid confusion or misinterpretation later. Using this list as a guideline for setting clear parameters will go a long way to ensuring your teams are set to succeed.

Chapter Fourteen Secrets

1. Establish the full team membership with clear parameters and operating standards.

2. Assume that conflict will occur. Monitor team dynamics and step in, as appropriate, to address issues and reset parameters.

3. Reward early "wins" and give credit evenly and amply to all team members.

4. Insist on good teamwork and demand rigorous and creative thinking from all.

Chapter Fourteen Exercise

Have several members of an operational team complete the Executive Leader's Checklist for High-Performance Teams. What can you learn from their responses? If needed, re-establish the standards and parameters by clarifying any uncertainty for the members of the team.

Chapter Fifteen

{ READY TO LEAD AND SET TO SUCCEED! }

If you are about to enter your first executive position, or if you are interviewing for your next executive position, you will want to give this chapter special attention. It covers your first few months in the position. The way you enter a job is a strong indicator of how you will leave the position, so you want to get it right, right from the start. This chapter identifies what you should and should not do.

Change Initiatives

Ready? Set? Stop! You probably see a lot of things you want to fix in your new organization or executive position. Having done your homework, you probably have a long list of ideas to bring to the company or the organization. It is counterintuitive and hard to do, but you need to slow down. Hang onto your great ideas and stifle your desire to fix things. Your first and most important job upon entering this new position is to develop trust among your people, your staff, and your stakeholders.

Warning: Their jobs didn't start the day you walked in the door, so start by collecting data. For instance, review climate surveys, management assessments, and assessments about the functioning of systems. (Perhaps review what you learned about conducting an internal assessment from reading Chapter Two). From the information you gather, determine the changes or improvements that have been tried before and failed. Understand why they failed. Was it the wrong solution for the problem? Was it the "political will" of key stakeholders or the lack of support among key groups? Perhaps it was a lack of resources or skills that caused the failure. Whatever the reason, it is of utmost priority to your success as a leader that you learn the history of failed initiatives as well as initiatives and systems that worked well so that you can benefit from that knowledge in leading your change agenda.

Cultural Identity

At the very top of your "to do" list is to learn and understand the culture of the company or organization. I've seen many new executives ignore the established culture to their detriment. They don't understand the unwritten rules, the policies for getting work done, and/or the methods for achieving success. They fail to appreciate what is valued by the people who have been at the company for a long time.

Culture is not an easy thing to understand immediately. You need to look at behavior and ask questions about what is behind decisions. When you start getting answers like, "That is just the way things are done around here," you know that you've hit on culture. Culture takes a long time to change and it can bring down a leader like no other force. If the culture is misaligned, be realistic in recognizing how much time and effort it can take to change it. For example, IBM's Lou Gerstner took the better part of a decade to successfully alter the culture there. See Chapter Seven for a review of culture.

Turn Off the J

One of the best things you can do when you first enter an executive position is to "turn off the J." What does that mean? It means to withhold judgment. Many leaders have the ability to make quick, intuitive judgments. They are usually quick to make decisions and often quick to judge the worthiness of an idea, person, approach, or strategy. While this is an important and beneficial skill to have, it can be a negative one if you use it too soon. As a new executive, you don't need to show people how much you know. You don't need to put people in "their place," and you don't need to be right, especially not in the beginning. Initially, just collect information, learn about your surroundings, and learn "how things are done around here."

Remember, your number one priority when you take an executive position is to build trust and develop relationships. When you first enter the job, the work environment is like a field of land mines, and you don't know where they are buried. You don't know how much or where you can exert pressure that won't trigger an explosion. Building strong relationships is such a significant part of your position that it is critical to do your best to avoid these land mines. You can do this pretty easily just by withholding negative or critical comments. Because of "judging" messages sent via body language or facial expressions, be mindful of your behavior as well. Go ahead and have the thoughts, but tuck them away in a file in your head for future use. Contrary to what you may believe, you won't be showing how smart you are by blurting out a critical comment. I've done this and it backfires completely!

Years ago, I was being briefed about our programs by my team when I first arrived in Cambodia. The entire team managing the democracy and governance portfolio was sitting around the conference room table. I was at the head of the table. When the office director, a lawyer by training and a true humanitarian whose core values were justice and fairness, briefed us on the human rights program, it was out of sync with other human rights reports I had read on Cambodia. I felt he was not viewing the situation objectively. I believed he was overstating the impact of our modest program. I bluntly called him out on it. He got flustered and backpedaled. I lost a fair amount of trust that day and probably some credibility, too. He and his team had prepared to brief me. Now he was onstage, performing in front of his team. My comments were misplaced and mistimed. It was as if the theater critic shouted out criticism in the middle of the performance. The room was silent as the poor office director climbed sheepishly out of the hole into which I had pushed him. This is not how to begin in a new position!

First impressions are disproportionately important to future success. They are like superglue: just slight contact and it sticks! If you unknowingly insult someone's status or the organization's core values or introduce elements of uncertainty, your new staff may withhold their trust from you. Making a bad first impression is very hard to undo, and you may have an uphill battle in gaining their trust. So, be careful when you speak before you've built trust, as your staff may misinterpret your intentions and take a comment that you make as critical or unnecessary. Without trust, they may take a joke or an off-the-cuff comment the wrong way. The ripple effect of these kinds of impressions can be quite damaging. Your staff will read into your comments negativity that you did not intend. They may shy away from you or from giving you their ideas –you absolutely need these to succeed. So, turn off the J. Be genuinely positive. First impressions count!

Listen and Listen Some More

When you enter your new position, engage your staff, listen to what they say, and listen to what is behind or underneath their words. What are their concerns? Impediments? Interests? Ideas? You may want to jot down notes or a list to refer to later. You want to engage your staff, your internal stakeholders, in helping you understand the existing vision and strategy. Ask them to conduct the internal and external assessments, and have them draw conclusions. Have them discuss the strengths and weaknesses of the company or organization. Engage them in shaping the new, revised, or revalidated vision. They want to engage. They will be thrilled that you want their ideas, their opinions, and their thoughts.

Capitalize on the energy that is created when you, a new leader, come into the organization and engage everyone possible! You may have to establish transition teams, issue-based foci, unit analysis, or other groupings to pull everyone into the vision and strategy-setting process. You will need to establish the process of how the groups will relate to one another and how the results of these groups will go into creating a vision. Be clear about how the external and internal analysis, conclusions, and ideas will lead to the formation of the vision and strategy.

When and how will your input as leader be woven into the work of staff and other leaders in the company or organization? It's pretty simple. You will set a timeline for accomplishing the review and analysis. How long an institution needs to conduct this kind of review depends on a host of factors, such as:

- *Size:* Larger organizations may need more time.

- *Geographic location:* Is everyone at one location? Are the offices within the U.S., or are they spread across the globe?

- *Data Availability:* Some organizations collect and analyze data regularly; others have never systematically collected the kind of data needed for internal and external analyses.

- *History:* What were the circumstances for the previous leader's departure?

- *Culture:* How accustomed are staff members to change and this kind of process?

- *Support of external stakeholders:* Whether a board of directors or Congress, how much support is there or will there be for a new or adjusted vision?

Engagement

The maximum amount of time a new leader of a large institution should take to conduct this kind of review is one year; the minimum time is six months. It simply takes that long for a new leader to build trust, learn the lay of the land, and engage staff in a meaningful way that will be useful in carrying out the vision, strategy, and accompanying change agenda.

If you are on the job for a month or two and you have developed the vision, I would question whether you have the level of engagement needed to implement the strategy and fulfill the vision. I would question whether your analyses (both external and internal) are broad and deep enough. I would question whether you have the political support you need to lead the vision.

One test is to ask, "Whose vision is it?" If the answer is "mine," then you haven't engaged others sufficiently. The vision needs to be owned by the staff. They also need to understand the strategy. Their sweat equity needs to be in the development of the vision and strategy, and the strategy needs to be consistent with the culture of the company or organization. The staff needs to believe it is possible. Only then will you have a chance of success.

Another test of the vision is to go to the edge of the enterprise, whether that be the sales force, accountants, or support staff, and ask them questions, like: "What is the new vision? What is the strategy? What is your role in achieving the vision?" If they can't answer any of these questions, then you know you have more work to do to engage people.

Initially, you'll want to limit the number of initiatives you plan to tackle. There is nothing worse than having a new boss who issues new initiatives without any sense of how much work they create. If you are adding new initiatives, then take away something else to leave a net of no additional time requirements. Create early wins and reward people, and you'll find that team spirit will carry them to the next set of initiatives. The momentum of challenge, achievement, success, and reward will lead them to put forward additional changes or challenges to tackle if you, as the executive, provide the space and the environment they need.

Tap Social Networks

Part of engaging staff is taking the time to understand their social networks. No, I don't mean Twitter or Facebook. I mean who influences whom at work, irrespective of the hierarchy. Sometimes you have a staff member nestled deep in the organization who actually wields a fair amount of influence over the other staff. Sometimes there is a gatekeeper. If you can build trust with her, the gates will open and many people will support you. We all know people like this in an organization. Sometimes they are the wise elderly person who works quietly behind the scenes to make things happen. Sometimes it is the guy who runs the office football pool. Sometimes it is the woman who always seems to have someone at her desk. Maybe it is a car pool or a group that goes fishing together who hold influence in ways that you, as the leader cannot see, unless you know to look.

Regardless of who they are, it is important to be aware of and understand the social networks and the influential people in your institution, for these can be powerful change agents if you win their trust and gain their support. On the other hand, if you are oblivious to these networks, their members, and their leaders, you are setting yourself up for failure. Just as they can be helpful to forming and achieving the vision, implementing the strategy, and carrying out the change agenda, they can work against you if you are unable to tap into their influence. Social networks are gold mines of information and influence and it behooves you to learn how to mine for gold!

Learning What They Take for Granted

While your groups or teams are conducting the internal assessment and reviews, you should spend your time learning things your staff already knows. In addition to the social networks, familiarize yourself with what forms the "backbone" of the organization or company. These are the things that tend to run throughout the institution; if one of these is missing or out of place; the entire company or organization will feel the pain. Sometimes these are interdependent systems. They can run across departments or units or they might be the "super systems," i.e., the things that, if changed or affected, have company-wide consequences. Table 15.1 is a checklist to uncover an organization's or company's "backbone."

Table 15.1: Questions to Unearth the Backbone of the Organization	
1	Checks and balances: How do decisions made in one department or business unit affect other departments? For instance, do program/product decisions affect the finance department, procurement decisions affect products or programs, or legal decisions impact finance or policy?
2	Governance system: How is policy made? How are rules established or eliminated?
3	Lines of authority: Who has authority over what and/or whom? How does accountability affect the organization or company?
4	Process of decision making: How are decisions made? What is the process for establishing delegations influencing training? What are the channels of dissent?
5	Accountability: What are the ways the system holds the other systems or people accountable?
6	Personnel system: What are the rewards and how are people promoted? (This is perhaps the most powerful system influencing other systems.)
7	Learning loops: What is the process of continual learning from actions, programs, and policies? How are adjustments made from lessons learned?

Make sure that your teams are working well together by doing periodic checkups. Think of the GPS that requires annual updating to take into account new streets, housing or construction, and name changes. Similarly, teams, even well-functioning and high-performing teams, need periodic check-ins and checkups. Your job is to make sure the team is heading in the right direction in an efficient manner.

Personal Board of Directors

Create a personal board of directors. Everyone who has served at or near the top of a company or organization has experienced loneliness. We've all heard the old saying, "It's lonely at the top." It's true! Expectations are high. You don't feel like you can go to your boss with a problem or issue for fear she will think that you don't know how to solve or approach a problem. This is not unusual, especially if you have infrequent contact with the big bosses. They expect you to take care of problems. In government, between political administrations, it is common to go a year or more without the confirmation of the full complement of executive leaders. In the private sector, you might meet with your board annually. Even if you felt you could discuss what's happening, your time with them is so infrequent that it probably won't help. You may also feel like you can't turn to your subordinates, even if they are part of your C-suite, because you don't want them to think you are in over your head or there may be issues too sensitive to discuss.

Who do you turn to if you have a "wicked" problem, for example, where they may be no right answers? I strongly suggest you create a personal board of directors or advisory council. Your personal board/council is made up of people that you feel you can call to discuss the challenges you face.

How do you create such a personal board and who should be on it? As an executive leader, keep in mind that the thorniest problems are reserved for you. After input from staff, you alone will make the decision and will likely be held to account for it. So, for your board, you want a group of people who don't think like you. This is counterintuitive on the surface. It is natural to turn to people who know you, think like you, even look like you, or have had similar experiences as you. However, you want to be able to call on people who bring different perspectives to the problem.

For example, if your view is primarily a technical one, you will want someone on your board or council who looks at problems from a political perspective, a perspective of tradition, and a perspective of impacts on people. The solution will need to encompass broad perspectives like technical, political, and cultural as well as be feasible.

If you tend to make decisions based on logic, rationale, or efficiency, then you will want someone on your board who looks at how decisions impact groups at a personal level. You'll want someone who knows how to get input and arguments from people who will help you make decisions. You may find more long-term benefits to making a decision that takes into account the personal impact of decisions.

If you are a conceptual thinker who can easily draw conclusions and judgments from a set of facts, then you will want someone on your board who is detail-oriented. This person will help you see the implications of your decision and will provide thinking on the feasibility of the decision based on details.

It is extremely helpful to have at least one personal board member who has walked in your shoes, knows your job, and has learned from mistakes.

Finally, you will want to have a trusted advisor or an executive coach who will be a thought partner in your decision making, i.e., someone who can ask questions to challenge your thinking. This person can help you reframe an issue or problem and examine it from multiple angles. She can also help you think through the implications of difficult conversations you may need to have or presentations you may need to make.

Establishing a board of directors or a personal advisory council with varied expertise is an excellent way to reduce the "loneliness at the top" feeling, obtain outside perspectives, benefit from others' experience, and be confident in your decisions.

Your First Address

One of your most important first steps as a new executive or leader in an organization or company is your first speech, town hall, or large meeting. There is a tremendous amount of pressure on you to lay out the new vision, strategy, and initiatives of your leadership. Many staff, especially more junior staff, will expect it. They will want definite answers or statements about top-line issues.

Again, it may be somewhat counterintuitive, but you will be best served if you keep your first remarks brief, vague, and personal. Refrain from talking about vision, strategy, or new initiatives except in very general and vague terms. It is too early. Remember the field of land mines. You don't know enough yet to avoid the pressure spots. You are in hyperlearning mode right now. You don't want to discourage anyone's engagement by delivering messages about the future. It is hard, especially for an experienced leader, to hold back, but resist the temptation to divulge your thinking, findings, or marching orders at this first meeting.

If you aren't discussing vision, strategy, and initiatives, except in very vague terms, what do you talk about at your initial town hall or staff meeting? Remember, you are in listening mode. Convey that you are taking the time to understand issues, people, culture, and strengths. Communicate that you want to build on what is already great and effective, and what has already been achieved by the organization. Tell people that you want to hear their concerns and ideas, and that you will be establishing groups and a process for gathering these so that you can take them into account moving forward. Relate to them as people with families, children, parents, siblings, and lives outside of work, not just as employees. The general theme should be: "I need you; I value you; I am new, you can teach me; I don't have all the answers; I need your ideas." You want to portray the message of shared ownership of the institution or organization. It is okay to show a little vulnerability and humility; these will contribute to the building of the trust that you will need to make any changes down the line.

If you have marching orders or a mandate, refer to them only in vague terms, regardless of whether they have been given to you by the board of directors, president, secretary, or your boss. Don't get me wrong: it is important to know and acknowledge your mandate and the parameters of your job. It is important to know why you were hired, what your higher-ups are looking to you to "fix." However, for your first meeting, you don't need to divulge the particulars to a large group. The risk of stepping on a land mine is too high. Table the details for now.

Chances are that anxiety levels among staff are high. New leadership almost always means change, and most people don't like change. Some people will be worried about their job security, their program, or their authority. Recognize their uncertainty. Let them know that uncertainty is a necessary step to get to certainty (vision and strategy) and that you are counting on their assistance and support. Essentially, you are asking for their help. Most people like to be asked to help. And most people like to help. It is hard to go wrong here.

Don't forget that what you say is as important as how you say it. The order in which you present is important; who you thank or acknowledge is important. Also, what you don't say, who you don't acknowledge, and who you don't thank are just as important in this first session.

Keep that in mind as you prepare your remarks. And you should prepare these remarks, even if you have a communications director and speechwriter. This first one should be from you, by you, and all you.

Finally, keep the first big meeting, town hall, or all-hands speech short. In all likelihood, someone else set up the meeting and established the parameters. Remember, you are in learning mode. Use this first big gathering to do just that. What can you learn about the authority, power, and culture of the company? Who is sitting on stage or near the podium with you? Who else speaks? What is the reaction from the crowd? Are people allowed to ask questions? Who answers them? What time of day is the first meeting? Is it mandatory? Learn all you can by observing how this institution runs this meeting before you put your fingerprints on it.

Protect Your Daily Reflection Time

I want to end this chapter with the notion of reflection. As noted in Chapter Eleven, reflection is thinking. You do it; everyone does it. However, as an executive leader, your success depends on it. It allows you to assimilate and synthesize information and to connect the dots in your conceptual framework. More than anything else, it is important to think and reflect right from the start, and you should establish this as a daily habit if you haven't already.

I know you are busy, but thinking and reflecting is your job. Ideally, block off time every day to do nothing but think. Not read, not write, sign documents, read briefs, or prepare for your daily meetings— just simply think.

What do you think about? Think about the analysis of the data from external and internal environments. Think about the vision and the culture. Think about your varied communications, audiences, stake-holders, messages, and messengers. How will you approach individuals and groups? What words will you use to elicit the desired outcomes? Think about problems and issues. Think about how your personal board or advisory council would approach or think about the problem and solutions. Think about your people and the meetings that you will have with them to provide feedback, pat them on the back, or guide them.

It takes tremendous skill base and years of experience to individualize messages and guide employees. It is easy to give them the answer; it is much harder to guide them in coming up with the answers themselves. It is difficult to hold back and allow people to fail or make mistakes. When they do so, help them get up, dust themselves off, pick up where they left off, and move forward. It is easy, even cowardly, to move employees who "don't get it" or who have "derailing" behaviors to the side. It is the executive leader who can work with these staff members, help them learn and develop behaviors more conducive to the achievement of the vision, who exhibits uncommon courage.

It takes a lot of executive-level skills to allow the space for "failure" and to stand by people as they learn and become more knowledgeable and resilient. All of these aspects of your job take regular thinking and reflection. And, here is the rub: if you, as the executive leader, are not thinking and reflecting, then you aren't learning. And you can bet no one else in the organization is reflecting, because they are too busy, as well. But you can bet your competitors are, and they will have the advantage.

Right from the start, set aside time every day for reflection. Treasure that time. Do not let anyone encroach on that space. It is, perhaps, the most critical investment you will make each day.

Summary

You now have the tools and knowledge to ensure that you are ready to lead and set to succeed. Take your time, build trust, engage staff, spend time every day reflecting, and reach out to others regularly for advice and input about the difficult issues that you will, no doubt, face. And finally, carefully craft your first address to your company or organization. Trust building officially begins with this speech, so be brief and sincere.

Chapter Fifteen Secrets

1. Take the time to understand the institutional culture.

2. Turn off the "J." Withhold judgment; first impressions are often wrong.

3. Slow down and take the time to build trust with your staff. You will need that trust capital to implement the change agenda.

4. Engage staff in shaping your understanding of issues; buy-in begins early.

5. Set a realistic timeline for review and analysis before drawing conclusions.

6. Limit the number of change initiatives you plan to tackle.

7. Create a personal board of directors and regularly call on them for guidance.

8. Invest in an executive coach who can help guide your transition to your new position.

9. Personally prepare your first address.

10. Use the first meeting, town hall, public address, or "all-hands" meeting to gather data.

11. Reserve time every day to think and reflect about issues, approaches, synthesizing disparate data, communications, and relationships.

Chapter Fifteen Exercise

List five to seven people that you would like to have on your personal board of directors and ask each of them to serve for a period of two years to help ensure you have the support you need to succeed. If you don't already have an executive coach, contact the International Coach Federation (coachfederation.org) for a roster of potential candidates.

Chapter Sixteen

{ THE PATH TRAVELED }

Executives today face a world more complex than has ever been seen. There is more information and greater uncertainty to be managed within fewer boundaries, calling for greater creativity, flexibility, and resiliency. The convergence of these factors is challenging, even for the best of leaders. Competition is stiff, and significant competitive advantages now come from factors that in the past provided only small incremental gains. Talent is more difficult to attract and retain, and in the near future, the effort that will go into talent management is unlike anything any organization or company has put forward to date. Globalization is stretching our boundaries, and technological advances allow us to collect finer and finer details of information to use in all areas of business. These kinds of advances are helping us to make better-informed decisions. They don't take the emotion out of decision making, but they do help to reduce the risk by accounting for personal biases and removing some of the guesswork. As part of these changes, leadership development has gained, and will continue to gain, focus.

Greater focus will be put on how well the organization functions, which is primarily the responsibility of its leaders. Individual accountability will rise. The technological tools available will be able to quantify and qualify individual contributions. This is already starting to happen with the wider acceptance and use of 360-feedback tools and increased transparency in using quantitative data to improve both individual and group performance. It's not enough to say a target was missed. Now we will know why it was missed. We'll be able to tell when it started going off course, so that midcourse corrections can be made sooner and with greater accuracy. Companies are using individualized learning tools like executive coaching to drive performance, and the government is learning the power of internal and external coaching.

As a result, learning will happen sooner, faster, and more methodically. This is good news if your ego can handle feedback. If you are able to bounce forward and learn, your chances of success will increase greatly. Resiliency is the key to success in the future, and not everyone has it. Further, not everyone who has it shares what they've learned. And as you've learned throughout this book, holding secrets will not only hurt your chances of leadership success, it will also be detrimental to your organization or company.

This goal of this book is to share secrets and share insights into the counterintuitive nature of leading at the executive level, to convey what you need to know to be a great executive. For those aspiring to lead at the highest levels, it is intended to prepare you. My hope is that by sharing this information, the examples, and my stories, you will be better prepared to lead. You will know more than I did when I was asked to lead. And hopefully, you'll make fewer mistakes than I did. In Sharing Secrets, I have shared mine with you in hopes of modeling vulnerability, a trait that I believe is critical for every great leader.

I have one last secret to share with you. The truth is that executive leadership is difficult and takes tremendous courage. It's hard because many aspects are not straightforward, but counterintuitive. Because of this, you will make mistakes along the way, and you will learn from them. Executive leadership takes courage, because as you make mistakes, you are on stage for all to see. You've got to say, "I don't know" sometimes or, "I need help." And rather than perceiving this vulnerability as a weakness, you must consider it a strength. Get comfortable with being vulnerable. Get to know yourself and let others know you. Be okay without knowing all the answers. Be humble, and put aside your ego. You will be called upon to meet incredible demands, and you'll need the self-confidence to push back when the demands are unreasonable (which sometimes, they will be). You've got to do the right thing all the time without exception. And, you've got to remain positive in the face of bad news and adversity. When you're wrong, which you will be sometimes, you have to say, "My judgment was wrong," or "I stand corrected." Sometimes you'll have to say, "There is no good answer" or "There are many right answers." You may have to say, "We can't get there from here." After you've tried your hardest and done your best and not met the success you expected, you have to reassess. Then you pick yourself up and dust yourself off to lead another day. Above all else, you must have the courage to take care of your people. It is your most important job to help them learn and grow, to help them develop resiliency when they make mistakes, and to help them redirect with a renewed sense of self-confidence.

I want to conclude with a glimmer of what it feels like when you have become vulnerable, dealt with fears, acknowledged mistakes, revealed embarrassing moments, discussed weaknesses, and embraced imperfections. That is when you know you are on track to reach your potential. That is when you know you've made it. It is when you obtain peace. I will leave you with this list of the qualities of inner peace presented by an unknown author. I wish you inner peace and fulfillment in all your executive leadership positions.

- An unmistakable ability to enjoy each moment

- Loss of interest in judging others

- Loss of interest in judging self

- Loss of interest in interpreting actions of others

- Loss of interest in conflict

- Loss of ability to worry

- Frequent, overwhelming episodes of appreciation

- Contented feelings of connectedness with others and nature

- Frequent attacks of smiling through the eyes from the heart

- Tendency to let things happen rather than make them happen

- Tendency to think and act spontaneously rather than from fear based on past expectations

- Susceptibility to love extended by others as well as the uncontrollable urge to extend love.

{ ABOUT THE AUTHOR }

A proven leader in executive coaching and organizational development, Erin Soto is a seasoned executive with more than 30 years of experience leading around the globe. She has dedicated her life to public service, first as a teacher, then as a Peace Corps Volunteer in Guatemala, then with the US Agency for International Development (USAID). She has lived and worked in Latin America, Africa, and Asia in Mali, Senegal, Haiti, Peru, Cambodia, and India. As a member of the Senior Foreign Service Office, she led programs as broad ranging as health and education, environment conservation, counter narcotics, agriculture, governance, energy, and innovation. As an assistant professor of behavioral science for the prestigious National Defense University, Erin taught strategic leadership and coached rising executives from across the national security sector and private industry.

More recently through her business, TLC Solutions, Erin offers expert assistance in organizational development and executive coaching. She is an ICF-certified executive coach and works with senior leaders and executives in both the public and private sector. She combines her academic foundation and extensive leadership experience with her coaching practice in TLC Solutions. Tailored solutions that exceed client expectations are the hallmark of TLC Solutions' success. Erin's focus is ensuring senior women are prepared to lead and set to succeed in executive positions.

Author of *Sharing Secrets: A Conversation about the Counterintuitive Nature of Executive Leadership*, Erin is a noted speaker on aspects of leadership.

Born in 1960 in Roswell, New Mexico. She is one of 13 siblings reared in an Irish Catholic family with socially conscious parents who were educators and civil rights activists. Her formative years were spent in Terre Haute, Indiana where she thrived in school government and athletics. Erin earned an undergraduate degree from the University of Wisconsin and a Masters from the George Washington University. She is married to Ben Soto and they have a daughter, Maggie and a son, Pedro.

{ BIBLIOGRAPHY }

Abramson, Mark A., Jonathan D. Breul, John M. Kamensky, and Martin G. Wagner, eds. *Getting It Done: A Guide for Government Executives*. Lanham, MD: Rowman & Littlefield, 2008.

---. *The Operator's Manual for the New Administration*. Lanham, MD: Rowman & Littlefield, 2008.

Aldrich, Gary. *Unlimited Access: An FBI Agent inside the Clinton White House*. Washington, DC: Regnery, 1996.

Amen, Daniel G. *Change Your Brain, Change Your Body: Use Your Brain to Get and Keep the Body You Have Always Wanted*. New York: Harmony Books, 2010.

---. *Change Your Brain, Change Your Life: The Breakthrough Program for Conquering Anxiety, Depression, Obsessiveness, Anger, and Impulsiveness*. New York: Times Books, 1998.

Ariely, Dan. *Predictably Irrational: The Hidden Forces That Shape Our Decisions*. New York: HarperCollins, 2008.

Axelrod, Richard H. *Terms of Engagement: New Ways of Leading and Changing Organizations*. 2nd ed, rev. and expanded. San Francisco: Berrett-Koehler, 2010.

Blank, Warren. *The 108 Skills of Natural Born Leaders*. New York: AMACOM, 2001.

Bolman, Lee G., and Terrence E. Deal. *Reframing Organizations: Artistry, Choice, and Leadership*. 5th ed. San Francisco: Jossey-Bass, 2013.

Boyatzis, Richard E., and Annie McKee. *Resonant Leadership: Renewing Yourself and Connecting with Others through Mindfulness, Hope, and Compassion*. Boston: Harvard Business Review Press, 2005.

Bradach, Jeffrey. *Organizational Alignment: The 7-S Model*. Boston: Harvard Business School Press, 1996.

Brafman, Ori, and Rod A. Beckstrom. *The Starfish and the Spider: The Unstoppable*

Power of Leaderless Organizations. New York: Portfolio, 2006.

Brown, Brené. Daring Greatly: *How the Courage to Be Vulnerable Transforms the Way We Live, Love, Parent, and Lead*. New York: Penguin, 2012.

---. The Gifts of Imperfection: *Let Go of Who You Think You're Supposed to Be and Embrace Who You Are*. Center City, MN: Hazelden, 2010.

Bruce, Anne, and James S. Pepitone. *Motivating Employees*. New York: McGraw-Hill, 1999.

Buckingham, Marcus, and Curt Coffman. *First, Break All the Rules: What the World's Greatest Managers Do Differently*. New York: Simon & Schuster, 1999.

Cameron, Julia. *The Right to Write: An Invitation and Initiation into the Writing Life*. New York: Jeremy P. Tarcher/Putnam, 1998.

Conference Board of Canada. *Capitalizing on Complexity: Insights from the Global Chief Executive Officer Study*. Ottawa: Conference Board of Canada, 2010.

---. Working Beyond Borders: *Insights from the Global Chief Human Resource Officer Study*. Ottawa: Conference Board of Canada, 2011.

Corvette, Barbara A. Budjac. *Conflict Management: A Practical Guide to Developing Negotiation Strategies*. Upper Saddle River, NJ: Prentice Hall, 2006.

Covey, Stephen R. *The 7 Habits of Highly Effective People: Powerful Lessons in Personal Change*. New York: Simon & Schuster, 1989.

Daly, Peter H., and Michael Watkins, with Cate Reavis. *The First 90 Days in Government: Critical Success Strategies for New Public Managers at All Levels*. Boston: Harvard Business School Press, 2006.

Firestien, Roger L. *Why Didn't I Think of That? A Personal and Professional Guide to Better Ideas and Decision Making*. Williamsville, NY: Innovation Resources, 1998.

Fisher, Kimball. *Leading Self-Directed Work Teams: A Guide to Developing New Team Leadership Skills*. Rev. and expanded ed. New York: McGraw-Hill, 2000.

Fisher, Roger, William L. Ury, and Bruce Patton. *Getting to Yes: Negotiating Agreement without Giving In*. 2nd ed. New York: Penguin, 1991.

Florida, Richard L. *The Flight of the Creative Class: The New Global Competition for Talent*. New York: HarperBusiness, 2005.

Ford, Linda. *The Fourth Factor: Managing Corporate Culture*. Indianapolis: Dog Ear, 2007.

Friedman, Thomas L. *Hot, Flat, and Crowded: Why We Need A Green Revolution—and*

How It Can Renew America. New York: Farrar, Straus and Giroux, 2008.

---. *The World Is Flat: A Brief History of the Twenty-First Century*. New York: Farrar, Straus and Giroux, 2005.

George, Bill, with Peter Sims. *True North: Discover Your Authentic Leadership*. San Francisco: Jossey-Bass, 2007.

Gladwell, Malcolm. *Blink: The Power of Thinking without Thinking*. New York: Little, Brown, 2005.

---. *Outliers: The Story of Success*. New York: Little, Brown, 2008.

---. *The Tipping Point: How Little Things Can Make a Big Difference*. New York: Little, Brown, 2000.

Goldsmith, Marshall, with Mark Reiter. *Mojo: How to Get It, How to Keep It, How to Get It Back If You Lose It*. New York: Hyperion, 2009.

Goleman, Daniel. *Social Intelligence: The New Science of Human Relationships*. New York: Bantam, 2006.

Goleman, Daniel, Richard E. Boyatzis, and Annie McKee. *Primal Leadership: Learning to Lead with Emotional Intelligence*. Boston: Harvard Business Review Press, 2004.

Grant, Adam. *Give and Take: Why Helping Others Drives Our Success*. New York: Penguin, 2013.

Greene, Bob, and Oprah Winfrey. *Make the Connection: Ten Steps to a Better Body— and a Better Life*. New York: Hyperion, 1996.

Hargrove, Robert A. *Masterful Coaching: Extraordinary Results by Impacting People and the Way They Think and Work Together*. New York: John Wiley & Sons, 1995.

Hyatt, Michael S. *Platform: Get Noticed in a Noisy World*. Nashville: Thomas Nelson, 2012.

Kaplan, Robert S., and David P. Norton. *Alignment: Using the Balanced Scorecard to Create Corporate Synergies*. Boston: Harvard Business School Press, 2007.

---. *The Balanced Scorecard*. Boston: Harvard Business School Press, 1996.

Katzenbach, Jon R., and Douglas K. Smith. *The Discipline of Teams: A Mindbook-Workbook for Delivering Small Group Performance*. New York: Wiley, 2001.

Kidder, Rushworth M. *How Good People Make Tough Choices: Resolving the Dilemmas of Ethical Living*. New York: HarperCollins, 1995.

Kotter, John P. *Leading Change*. Boston: Harvard Business School Press, 1996.

Lehrer, Jonah. *Imagine: How Creativity Works*. New York: Houghton Mifflin Harcourt, 2012.

Linden, Russell Matthew. *Working across Boundaries: Making Collaboration Work in Government and Nonprofit Organizations*. San Francisco: Jossey-Bass, 2002.

Lombardo, Michael M., and Robert W. Eichinger. *FYI: For Your Improvement: A Guide for Development and Coaching for Learners, Managers, Mentors, and Feedback Givers*. 5th ed. Los Angeles: Lominger International, 2009.

Magretta, Joan. *Understanding Michael Porter: The Essential Guide to Competition and Strategy*. Boston: Harvard Business School Press, 2012.

Maxwell, John C. *Developing the Leaders around You: How to Help Others Reach Their Full Potential*. Nashville: Thomas Nelson, 2003.

---. *Failing Forward: Turning Mistakes into Stepping-Stones for Success*. Nashville: Thomas Nelson, 2000.

---. *The 21 Irrefutable Laws of Leadership: Follow Them and People Will Follow You*. Nashville: Thomas Nelson, 1998.

May, Rollo. *The Meaning of Anxiety*. New York: Ronald Press, 1950.

Morgan, Howard J., Philip J. Harkins, and Marshall Goldsmith, eds. *The Art and Practice of Leadership Coaching: 50 Top Executive Coaches Reveal Their Secrets*. Hoboken, NJ: John Wiley & Sons, 2005.

Newell, Terry, Grant Reeher, and Peter Ronayne. *The Trusted Leader: Building the Relationships That Make Government Work*. Washington, DC: CQ Press, 2008.

Nilekani, Nandan. *Imagining India: The Idea of a Renewed Nation*. New York: Penguin, 2009.

Palmer, Jim. *The Magic of Newsletter Marketing: The Secret to More Profits and Customers for Life*. Exton, PA: Success Advantage, 2009.

Puccio, Gerard J., Mary C. Murdock, and Marie Mance. *Creative Leadership: Skills That Drive Change*. Thousand Oaks, CA: SAGE, 2007.

Rock, David, and Linda J. Page. *Coaching with the Brain in Mind: Foundations for Practice*. Hoboken, NJ: John Wiley & Sons, 2009.

Sashkin, Marshall, and Molly G. Sashkin. *Leadership That Matters: The Critical Factors for Making a Difference in People's Lives and Organizations' Success*. San Francisco: Berrett-Koehler, 2003.

Sheahan, Peter. Flip: *How to Turn Everything You Know on Its Head—and Succeed Beyond Your Wildest Imaginings*. New York: HarperCollins, 2008.

Silsbee, Douglas K. The Mindful Coach: *Seven Roles for Facilitating Leader Development*, new and rev. ed. Foreword by Marshall Goldsmith. San Francisco: Jossey-Bass, 2010.

Thomas, Martin. *Loose: The Future of Business Is Letting Go*. London: Headline, 2011.

Tracy, Brian. *How the Best Leaders Lead: Proven Secrets to Getting the Most out of Yourself and Others*. New York: AMACOM. 2010.

Underhill, Brian O., Kimcee Lee McAnally, and John J. Koriath. *Executive Coaching for Results: The Definitive Guide to Developing Organizational Leaders*. San Francisco: Berrett-Koehler, 2007.

Vroom, Victor H., and Phillip W. Yetton. *Leadership in Decision-Making*. PA: University of Pittsburgh Press, 1973.

Yukl, Gary A. *Leadership in Organizations*, 8th ed. Englewood Cliffs, NJ: Prentice-Hall, 2012.

{ FOOTNOTES }

Chapter 1

1. Arnsten, A.F., "Stress signaling pathways that impair prefrontal cortex structure and function," National Review of Neuroscience, 2009, June:10 (6):410-422. doi:10.1038/nrn2648.

2. Phil Harkins, "Powerful Conversations: How High-Impact Leaders Communicate," in *The Structure and Impact of Powerful Conversations* (New York: McGraw-Hill, 1999), 19-41.

Chapter 2

3. Admiral Mike Mullen, "How to Lead," Interview broadcast on Fareed Zakaria GPS, CNN, December 23, 2010), http://www.cnn.com/video/data/2.0/video/us/2010/12/23/gps.leadership.mullen.cnn.html.

4. Jim Collins, "First Who...Then What," in *From Good to Great: Why Some Companies Make the Leap...and Others Don't,* (New York: HarperBusiness, 2001), 42-64.

5. Rebecca Glicksberg Skipper, "Third Culture Kids: Growing up Abroad Offers Advantages," *Transitions Abroad Magazine*, 1, www.transitionabroad.com/publications/magazine/0009/third_culture_kids.shtml.

6. Brené Brown, "Debunking the Vulnerability Myths ," in *Daring Greatly: How the Courage to Be Vulnerable Transforms the Way We Live, Love, Parent, and Lead* (New York: Penguin, 2012), 47.

Chapter 3

7. Thomas H. Kean, Final Report of the National Commission on Terrorist Attack (9/11 Commission Report Executive Summary), (Washington, DC: Government Printing Office, July 2004), page 16.

8. Nate Collins (retired President and Chairman of the Board, BancTexas), interviewed by the author, April 15, 2014.

9. Fumio Kodama, "Technology Fusion and the New R&D," *Harvard Business Review Global Editions*, July 1992, http://hbr.org/1992/07/technology-fusion-and-the-new-rd/ar/1.

10. Ibid.

Chapter 4

11. Albert S. Humphrey, "SWOT Analysis for Management Consulting," *SRI Alumni Newsletter*, December 2005, http://www.sri.com/sites/default/files/brochures/dec-05.pdf.

12. Michael E. Porter, "The Five Competitive Forces That Shape Strategy" *Harvard Business Review*, January 2008.

13. Joan Magretta, *Understanding Michael Porter: The Essential Guide to Competition and Strategy* (Boston: Harvard Business School Press, 2012), 35-61.

14. Robert S. Kaplan and David Norton, *The Balanced Scorecard*, (Boston: Harvard Business School Press), 1996.

Chapter 5

15. Bob McDavid, President of McDavid, Inc, email correspondence, 11/22/13, www.mcdavidusa.com.

16. Albert Humphrey, "SWOT Analysis for Management Consulting," *SRI Alumni Newsletter*, www.sri.com, 2005, 7-8.

17. Michael E. Porter, "The Five Competitive Forces That Shape Strategy," *Harvard Business Review*, January 2008, 2-17.

18. Robert S. Kaplan and David P. Norton, *Alignment: Using the Balanced Scorecard to Create Corporate Synergies*, (Boston: Harvard Business School Press, 2007), 36-39.

19. Jeffrey Bradach, "Organizational Alignment: The 7-S Model," Harvard Business School, Product Number 9-497-045, 1996, 1-8

20. R.H. Waterman, T.J. Peters, and J.R. Phillips, "Structure Is Not an Organization," *Business Horizons*, 1980, 17-25.

Chapter 6

21. Michael Beer and Nitin Nohria "Cracking the Code" *Harvard Business Review*, May-June 2000, 15.

22. Gary Yukl, "Leading Change in Organizations," in *Leadership in Organizations*, 8th ed. (Englewood Cliffs, NJ: Prentice Hall, 2012), 302.

23. A.E. Rafferty and M.A. Griffin, "Perceptions of Organizational Change: A Stress and Coping Perspective," *Journal of Applied Psychology*, 2006, 91 (5), 1154-1162.

Chapter 7

24. Edgar H. Schein, "How Leaders Embed and Transmit Culture," in *Organizational Culture and Leadership*, 4th edition, (San Francisco: Jossey-Bass, 2010), 235-258.

25. Charles A. O'Reilly and Jennifer A. Chatman, "Culture as Social Control: Corporations, Cults, and Commitment," Research in Organizational Behavior, 1996, 18, 4.

26. Linda Ford, *The Fourth Factor: Managing Corporate Culture* (Indianapolis, IN: Dog Ear Publishing, 2007).

Chapter 8

27. David Rock and Linda J. Page, *Coaching with the Brain in Mind*, (Hoboken, New Jersey: John Wiley & Sons, Inc.) 2009, 443-445.9

28. Jenny Vernooy, Ian Maxwell, Leslie Reed, Bill Gelman and their Peruvian counterparts were all part of these efforts.

Chapter 9

29. Thomas Owen Jacobs, "Leader Development," in *Strategic Leadership: The Competitive Edge* (Washington, D.C: National Defense University, Industrial College of the Armed Forces, 2002), 84-85.

30. Daniel Goleman, Richard E. Boyatzis, and Annie McKee, *Primal Leadership: Learning to Lead with Emotional Intelligence*, (Boston: Harvard Business School Press, 2004), 38.

31. Ibid. 3.

32. Victor H. Vroom and Phillip W. Yetton, *Leadership in Decision-Making* (PA: University of Pittsburgh Press, 1973).

33. Andrew Campbell and Jo Whitehead, "How to Test Your Decision-Making Instincts," *McKinsey Quarterly*, May 2010, 1-3.

34. Rushworth M. Kidder, *How Good People Make Tough Choice: Resolving the Dilemmas of Ethical Living*, (New York: HarperCollins, 1995).

Chapter 10

35. Jonah Lehrer, "The Eureka Hunt: Why Do Good Ideas Come to Us When They Do?" *New Yorker*, July 28, 2008, 40-45.

36. Amy Arnsten, Rajita Sinha, and Carolyn M. Mazure, "This Is Your Brain in Meltdown" *Scientific American*, April 2012, 49-53.

37. Stephen R. Covey, *The 7 Habits of Highly Effective People: Powerful Lessons in Personal Change* (New York: Simon & Shuster, 1989), 288-289.

38. Ibid., 287.

39. Marshall Goldsmith with Mark Reiter, *Mojo: How to Get It, How to Keep It, How to Get It Back If You Lose It* (New York: Hyperion, 2009), 84-86.

40. Anne Marie Slaughter, "Why Women Still Can't Have It All," *Atlantic*, July-August 2012. http://m.theatlantic.com/magazine/archive/2012/07/why-women-still-cant-have-it-all/309020/.

Chapter 11

41. J.M. Schwartz, H.P. Stapp, and M. Beauregard, "A Neurophysical Model of the Mind-Brain Interaction." *Philosophical Transactions of the Royal Society* B: Biological Sciences, 360, 1458.

42. Michael M. Lombardo & Robert W. Eichinger, *FYI: For Your Improvement: A Guide for Development and Coaching for Learners, Managers, Mentors, and Feedback Givers*, 5th ed. (Los Angeles: Lominger International), 2009.

Chapter 14

43. Adam Grant, "Givers Take All: The Hidden Dimension of Corporate Culture," *McKinsey Quarterly*, April 2013, 1-8.

44. Jon R. Katzenbach and Douglas K. Smith, "The Discipline of Teams," *Harvard Business Review*, July 2005. http://hbr.org/2005/07/the-discipline-of-teams/ar/1.

Made in the USA
San Bernardino, CA
05 February 2015